Giving Him Back to God
By Beth Baker

Copyright 2011 by Beth Baker

Chapter 1 - The Blessing

Chapter 2 - The Change

Chapter 3 - The Word Epilepsy

Chapter 4 - Fighting for Progress in Spite of Seizures

Chapter 5 - Losing Skills But Finding Hope

Chapter 6 - Finding Kindred Spirits

Chapter 7 - The Home Front

Chapter 8 - Surgery, School and Sleeplessness

Chapter 9 - Feeding, Frailty and Faith

Chapter 10 - Rolling With The Punches: G-tubes, GI and Ice Storms

Chapter 11 - Calm Waters and Agonizing Reality

Chapter 12 - Swinging, Facing the Music and Seeing through the Seizures

Chapter 13 - Changes, Regression and Hope

Chapter 14 - Making Memories and Managing Care

Chapter 15 - Blessings of Family

Chapter 16 - Giving Him Back to God

Chapter 17 - Lessons from Caleb's Journey

Dedication

This book is dedicated to the bravest, most beautiful child, Caleb Baker who taught me that this life is temporary at best but full of blessings and joys that can be found even in the darkest of days. I love you sweet boy.

Thanks

To my husband Chad, for standing beside me through it all.
To Peyton and Camille- for being wonderful sisters, and amazing young ladies, we are so proud of you both.
To my sister Ellen, my second set of hands and best friend.
To my family, all of you- we could not have made it through without each of you, we love you more than we can say.
To TEAM CALEB--for lifting us up in prayer and being there every moment.

Chapter 1: The Blessing

Every child is a blessing. Having a child with special needs to come into your life is an even bigger blessing. And losing that child who has brought so much joy into your life can break your being. I have no cross by the roadside to mark a tragic death, he died in my arms...they are forever with me, attached, a reminder every day of holding him close to my heart. And while he is no longer physically with us, his journey, his strength and his smile resonates in our being - every day.

Let me tell you about the child who made our lives so blessed.

Caleb Asher Baker was born on November 7, 2001. He was a healthy, chubby, little boy, weighing 9lbs. 6oz. He was beautiful. The only problem he had at the hospital was a case of jaundice, but sunshine through the windows helped his levels to drop quickly and we were able to bring him home.

His wonderful "big" sisters, Peyton and Camille were 4 and 2 at the time, and bundles of energy. After we had found out we were pregnant with number three, Chad, my husband and I were happy to see on the ultrasound that this sweet boy would bless our family with a good change. We were anticipating all the fun and rowdiness a little boy would bring to our home. We were so thankful that he was such a happy and healthy looking baby. So many expectations, dreams, anxieties and joy fill you when a new baby comes along. Chad had dreams for him, I was just busy spoiling him from the beginning, knowing he would be our last child. I was determined he would be "mommy's little boy."

He was a good baby. He rarely cried at all. He had trouble nursing though, and I wasn't making enough to help him gain the weight he needed. So we moved to bottles at about 2 months. He rarely even fussed, the only thing he cried about was a bath early on. This was a good thing, for at the time, my health was failing me. I became weak and tired chronically. I was having severe headaches and dizziness as well as a host of GI issues. However, the kids were happy and busy and I did my best to keep up with them. The girls loved playing with Caleb, they would play kitchen with him and dress him up. Bless his heart, he didn't care at all, he would just smile at them!

Caleb was a busy toddler, he would clean out the Tupperware cabinet in the kitchen and crawl inside the cabinet and shut the door. He was so sweet and would "peek a boo" out the door at us, we would say the words and he would smile and shut the door and peek out again. He could do this all day if I let him. He also liked to play with things that were not toys. After three children, this house would rival the best toy store. However, in a room full of age appropriate toys, Caleb would choose to play with the springs on the baby bed. It was odd, but I thought as a boy, maybe he was just going to be "mechanically minded". So I dismissed the odd behavior. He was after all, happy and healthy.

He did contract several upper respiratory illnesses early on in his first few years. Peyton, our oldest had started school so we had plenty of "bugs" that would find there way into our home. But for the most part, Caleb seemed to be developing okay. He was sitting up at 7 months, crawling well by 9, pulling up, and taking his first steps by 13 months. He was a bit on the slow end, but he was a boy and our baby, so I was usually carrying him and tending to his needs rather than making him "work" to gain what he wanted. Caleb had always had lots of drooling as a baby, we put a bib on him constantly just to keep his clothes underneath dry. And even then, often he would be just wet from drooling. We thought it was from teething. But, it continued past teething stages.

Caleb was developing pretty well in speech. He could say Mama, (the most important, of course!) and Dad-da, and Dog and Cat and Sissy and Juice, etc. He would point to things as if to ask, "What is that?" or to show me a bird out in the yard.

At 15 months, I noted in his baby book that he "quit talking". At the time, I recall thinking, well he is just being stubborn and would rather we bring him whatever he wants. But at 15 months, what child does that? Children at that age are just drinking in life, they are curious and happy and want to please their parents. They are modeling everything that their parents and siblings are doing. So this to me was odd. And it really didn't resonate with me that something could have been wrong. But little by little it became more and more evident that something was changing with Caleb.

Chapter 2: The Change

By 24 months, we knew something was just not right. Caleb could not communicate with us. He would run through the house all day and turn on/off the lights, shut doors, bang on windows, and do anything disruptive he could think of. I really didn't know what to do. I thought he was bored. I would try to play with him, but he was not interested. He would not watch television at all. But, he was a rough and tumbly, rowdy little boy. "Bubba" lovingly became his nickname by the girls and several in the family.

He would let me read to him, so I read all day long. Every once in a while he would repeat words I read, so this was a good thing for him. My health was failing me terribly, I would almost faint if I got up too quickly. So Caleb would go and get a book off the shelf and we would read all day. I would get the girls on the bus and lie on the couch to recover. Caleb would bring me his favorite "Mother Goose Nursery Rhymes" and our day would begin. I would sneak in some Dr. Seuss here and there, and sometimes if I stopped reading, he would even finish the phrase. So I felt we were making some progress.

By the time he was three his behavior had really become a problem. He would pull the girls hair and scream, he would hit and bite. We talked to our pediatrician, Dr. Jeffrey Mudd, about this and he recommended doing "time out" for him for 2 minutes and then see how Caleb responded. By the time two minutes were up it was clear he had no idea why he was sitting there. I told him one time to tell Camille "sorry I hit you" and he said "I pulled hair". While this was typically why he was in time out, it wasn't the case this time, and I realized at that moment, he was just repeating what I normally asked him to apologize for. He truly did not understand. Dr. Mudd recommended we have Caleb tested for developmental delay. It was a devastating blow, but he said exactly what I expected him to, I knew deep down that developmentally something was wrong. It was agonizing. We wanted so badly to help him, but I had no idea what to do or where to start.

We would have to wait 10 months before the testing center was able to schedule an appointment. This was a long 10 months. It was so frustrating for us and I could not imagine how frustrating it was for Caleb. It broke our hearts that he was not understanding us.

In February of 2005, I was finally diagnosed with Addison's disease, Hypothyroidism and Hypoglycemia. I started my daily regimen of medicine that truly seemed daunting at first. I was the type of person who took ½ of a Tylenol for a bad headache. But, I started feeling so much better. I was so grateful to have an answer for what was causing my illness and was thankful that it was treatable.

Now, my full attention could be focused on helping our sweet little boy, who was struggling. It was just heartbreaking. I tried everything I could to keep him engaged. We would try to do crafts with him, he liked to do finger paints some. But the only thing he would really play with was tools. He knew every kind of tool there was. He would hold them up, I would tell him what it was, and he memorized them. He would go through them over and over. If you asked for a crescent wrench he would hand you the right one every time. My dad, "Papa", and Caleb would go through his tool box and he would do the same. Caleb would just smile, it made him happy.

He also loved the outdoors. He would hear an airplane or helicopter outside way before I could hear anything and would say "Plane, plane!" And sure enough in a few moments, I would hear it. I figured he was just very perceptive. He was, but it was his very heightened sense of hearing that allowed him to tune in to things around him so well. He loved running around the backyard chasing our little dog "Abby." She was so sweet to him. Caleb could sit on her and she wouldn't flinch. She would put his hand in her mouth and lead him around the yard like her own little puppy. I think she knew something was different about Caleb. She was a good friend to him.

By summer of 2005, the Today Show on NBC had a series with Matt Lauer about the rising numbers of Autism and the symptoms. I watched. However, I was hoping that this wasn't Caleb. He had many of the classic symptoms, but some he did not have. Caleb typically could look at you in the eyes, not every time, but most of the time. He also was very affectionate and loved big hugs and for you to hold him. So in the back of my mind, I knew it was a possibility. I was just hoping that this was not where we were headed. However, the more I read, the more convinced I was that we were dealing with Autism.

I spoke to a teacher who was a classmate of mine, and she recommended I speak to the preschool teacher. We could possibly get Caleb enrolled before he had his "formal testing" based on the Head Start evaluation. Caleb failed the tests with flying colors. It broke my heart. I wanted so badly for him to be able to test just like my girls had for Kindergarten, but he did not understand what he was being asked to do. He was simply "not with us". I cried all the way home from testing and decided right then, we were going to do something, now.

I didn't know where to even begin, but after just a small bit of research I instructed everyone in our family that we were going to do things differently for Caleb and I needed them on board. Lucky for us, we have the most supporting and loving family there is, so we all changed how we talked to Caleb. We told him what "to do" not what "not to do". If he stood on the couch, a favorite past time of his, then we would simply say "feet down". After a minute he would obey and get down. I was seeing that it was taking him a long time to process what was said to him. His preschool teachers worked diligently with him and by September 8, 2005 he was formally diagnosed with PDD-NOS, Pervasive Development Disorder Not Other Wise Specified. This basically meant, Autism.

We had some basic testing done, for Fragile X syndrome, and then an elements hair study done, and then he was scheduled for a 20 minute EEG. This was by far the scariest for me. And I was so glad when it came back "OK". But with the Autism diagnosis, they handed me a packet that basically said "Your kid has Autism, good luck with that," and sent us on our way. In the back of the packet there was a page on "Dealing with Grief". I thought, "Seriously, why would I need that?" But a day later I knew why.

The flooding of emotion over dealing with autism was overwhelming. I had been in denial a long time, but had somewhat accepted it, I thought. However, the grief of knowing that your child will struggle, that your child may not be able to do all those things you had dreamed for them, knowing that others would not accept your child for who they are….that grief overcomes you and breaks your heart and leaves a mark.

I decided we were going to do as much as we possibly could to help Caleb. There is lots of information on the internet. But it is a maze. Some "treatments" are out and out lies. Some are tried and true helps. But regardless if they work at all for one child, they may not work for yours. There is no "test" to see what aids, programs, diets, vitamins, supplements, will best help your child. It is trial and error. And with time so precious, we got to work as soon as possible. I am all for the least intrusive treatments. So we started with a gluten free and casein free diet, mainly because Caleb dealt with diarrhea daily. I made sure that his foods were the same as what the other children were having each day. If it was hamburger day, Caleb would have a modified version of a hamburger, if it were pizza day, he had pizza. I didn't want him to feel like he was eating different than the other children were, so I analyzed the menu and prepared his meals to match every day. His teachers were excellent in helping us through the change. We also at that
same time began speech, occupational therapy and physical therapy at school and in an outpatient facility.

Autism changed our lives to some degree. My time was more focused on Caleb's learning and development, so the girls had to do without mama up at the school as the "room mom". It was an adjustment. Chad and I experienced the stress over the consuming time that it took just to get Caleb to be able to do a simple task. The only thing I could do was to pray for more patience, and try to teach everyone in our family how to interact with Caleb and to wait for him to attempt to respond. We were still taking Caleb to worship and to the store, etc. However, we didn't do anything without "preparing him first".

We modeled appropriate behavior at home. We began the Picture Exchange Communication System (PECS), and I was adamant that all staff working with him used it appropriately and across multiple settings. I started doing a mix of : Floortime, Relationship Development Intervention, TEACCH, Applied Behavior Analysis and had all of his teachers, aids and therapists on board. It was working.

He responded well to pictures and seemed to enjoy our activities together. He was happy, he was able to learn to ride a tricycle, his colors and loved the computer. He was learning to play with others and making friends, he was smiling....that meant the most

Chapter 3: The Word Epilepsy

One afternoon in late spring of 2006, Caleb's preschool teacher asked me if he'd been tested for Epilepsy. I recalled his EEG and said it came back fine, but I asked her why. She said "He just has days where he is fine and then the next moment he is "not with us"." She described what an absence seizure was, the staring off and disconnecting. I recalled that Caleb has done that off and on for years, since he was probably two I had noticed it. But typically he would be "zoned out" and could still manipulate a toy. (at the time he liked cars and would spin the wheels repetitively). She noted that he had a toy in his hand that he was spinning when she observed this absent-like behavior. I didn't know what to think.

We continued to work hard to develop speech and Caleb was making great gains. He was starting by summer of 2006 to be able to request his needs, like; " I want juice" or " I want to play". It was so encouraging. One day at naptime, I realized Caleb wanted his juice box, and typically Chad would bring it to us. I tried to get him to hear me from the other room, but he couldn't. Finally Caleb said "Chaaad, juice box"! I know he was just imitating me, but it was the cutest thing, and we were so happy that he had found a few words that were helping him.

I was also working on teaching him emotions I started with "happy and sad". One afternoon he asked for a "Squeeze" which was a big hug (typical for deep pressure seeking sensory kids). He picked up a truck to play with and said "I'm so very happy!" I cried with joy, my Caleb had said for the first time at age 5 how he felt. It was a beautiful moment!

Caleb was making progress, this was a first. We were hoping that this path would continue. I was hoping to take him for his reevaluation in September and hear them say he was improving, we certainly had hope! I remember thinking, Caleb could overcome this, and that was a great feeling.

July 4, 2006 changed our lives, and Caleb's. We were on our annual trip to the Paducah, KY riverfront to watch the firework display. We had stopped for drinks and Caleb had taken a sip of a slush. A few minutes later he started screaming.

Caleb had always been a rough playing kid, but nothing in his life had ever frightened him. He had fallen multiple times and cut his cheek or head. He wouldn't cry because of the pain, but because you had to hold him down to get the bleeding to stop. He had no fear of danger, no concept of hurt, but he was screaming. I could not figure out what was wrong. He was in his car seat in the back of the van, it was dark. Chad could not see anything visibly wrong. He screamed again. We had arrived at the riverfront, and Papa had come to the car to help with Caleb as he always did. I told him what was going on and asked if Chad and the girls could ride back with them and I was going to take Caleb back home. Something was just not right. We started home and the screaming began again. I couldn't get home fast enough. I picked him up and he was soaking wet. (Caleb was not yet potty trained) He was shaky and sweaty. I brought him inside. I put him on the couch and went to get a cool rag to wipe him down, I came back and he was asleep.

Caleb had not been a good sleeper since birth. He rarely took naps lasting more than 20 minutes. He rarely slept through the night. Over the past 4 years Caleb fought going to sleep every night. Music seemed to be the only way to get him to finally rest. So I was completely puzzled over what in the world he was screaming for, what scared him, what was the matter, and why did he just pass out afterward. I was very upset and worried that something more was wrong.

Three days later, on July 7th I witnessed the reason why he screamed on the 4th. Caleb rounded the corner into the kitchen to find me and was screaming. As soon as I touched him to pick him up he began violently shaking all over. There was no doubt in my mind, this was a seizure. It lasted over 10 minutes. I had the girls to call my mom, Nana and my sister, Ellen for help. I held Caleb in my arms, his limbs shaking uncontrollably, and more intensely. It slowed some and then it would pick up intensity again. His eyes met mine and he said "It's okay?", as for me to assure him that he would be okay, I lost it. It was not okay, this precious boy, who has struggled to speak is asking me if he is okay because he is fully aware that what is happening in his little brain is not okay. There are no words to describe the feeling of helplessness. All I could do was hold him and tell him "Mama will hold you".

We took him to the local hospital that did all of the standard tests to verify that there was not infection or fever causing the seizure. We were instructed to come back if it happened again. The next day he had two more partial seizures. So we took him back to the hospital and he was airlifted to a children's hospital in Louisville, Kentucky.

By the next morning we had seen about five Doctors. Many of them asked about his history, etc. we met the attending pediatric neurologist who observed Caleb and described him as having "high functioning autism". I figured because of Caleb's calm demeanor, eye contact and social skills that we had worked so intently on, he appeared "high functioning".

We discussed that Caleb now had Epilepsy. About two weeks before this I had read more on epilepsy when a dear friend lost her adult child who had seizures. I had read the statistics; 20% of children with autism will develop epilepsy; but I was praying that we would not be the 20%. Sadly, now we were.

Caleb was placed on Trileptal and we were sent home with instructions to wean up the dosage over time to help "cover" his seizure activity. His seizure numbers increased rapidly. He began wringing his hands together. We increased the Trileptal to help with the increase in seizures, but with that increase came lethargy. He would occasionally still be able to have words, on July 27th he said "Caleb wants to play", and on July 30th he said his sisters name "Peyton." With every word that he would say, we would have hope that more would come back. We just had to stop the seizures. I prayed every night for them to stop.

Chapter 4: Fighting for Progress in Spite of Seizures

During this time we had started an attempt at potty training, but with the seizure activity Caleb would have bouts of uncontrolled diarrhea especially right before seizure activity. So, we decided to back off of that goal for right now since Caleb had no control over this and it would likely be very frustrating for him. Some things that had seemed so important for him to accomplish were no longer goals. This was hard to deal with emotionally. When you want to see your child succeed, the last thing you want to see is them to struggle. Seizures were winning, but we were trying to fight harder.

His sleeping patterns were worse, and he was fighting me nightly in going to sleep. We started using Melatonin to help him relax enough to be able to fall asleep. I would turn on music sometimes to try to help as well. It was almost as though he were afraid to go to sleep. That was heartbreaking. He was very tired throughout his daytime activities and I felt like his cognition was diminishing as well.

By October 2006, we started Depakote to try to help with the seizure activity. Depakote is also used in patients with Autism Spectrum Disorders, and is thought to help them focus, so I was hopeful that this would help Caleb two-fold. He was still able to speak some but it was very sporadic. On October 1st, he said "scared" and then had a partial seizure. How was it that he could go for days without words and then these mean old seizures would bring out the saddest of words?

On the 4th though, he was able to say his name for the first time, "My name's Caleb Baker". It was a beautiful achievement, I was amazed then, as I am to this day, that he was able to formulate any words at all....but this was our Caleb, who was amazing every day! He was so smart, he just had trouble making the right connections to be able to express what he needed to. I wished for just a moment we could see what was going on inside his beautiful, magnificently made brain.

On the 29th of October he wanted to leave Nana's house, stood at the door, and said "I am so very sad". It was times like these that broke all of our hearts. He was very tired and worked so hard at all of his therapies. We had gone to Nana and Papa's house for a break from our house and he just could not handle the change. His routine was necessary and any deviation from that made him uncomfortable and he felt out of sorts. We worked on making a family card schedule then, so that when we were going to a new location we would have an appropriate picture with us to try to prepare him for the change. It helped tremendously.

For November, December and January of 2006/2007, we saw no "visible" seizures with Caleb. The depakote seemed to help him be more "present". But he was having extreme difficulty with napping and sleep. By February of '07 the seizures were back, he had a 5 minute seizure and we were instructed to take him to the hospital. They increased his Depakote levels and we noted that after three days of back to back seizures that he was having difficulty with balance and with swallowing food. This was so hard to see. It was one thing to deal with the Autism symptoms that seem to be exasperated by the seizures, but it was another to see him physically having deterioration of ability.

In March, after a long seizure and treatment with DiaStat (rectal valium) to stop the seizure, he had trouble again with balance and swallowing. At this point I wondered what part of the brain were these seizures coming from as they were effecting his mobility and ability to eat. His seizures began changing. He had multiple seizures back to back and from the research I could do, I truly felt like he was experiencing Frontal Lobe seizures now. He was exhausted after them, and the light in his eyes would be gone, there was just sadness in them that ate at my heart.

We were also having trouble finding therapists that could work successfully with Caleb and understand that he would not be able to be consistent. We did have a wonderful Occupational Therapist, that was great with Caleb. She adopted our visual schedule for him and did water therapy with him to help calm him. It helped him greatly at the time and allowed him to focus better when asked to work. She was very good with him and understood that every day for him was different. What he could do one day, he might not be able to the next.

Topamax was added to his regimen for seizures at the beginning of April. He became extremely lethargic, would sleep for up to 4 hours during the day. His speech was diminishing even more. I called the Neurologist at Louisville and we took him off the Topamax and did a 23 hour EEG that showed NOTHING. They added Keppra to his regimen and we took him back home. And the seizures returned, with a vengeance.

Chad and I had taken the girls to Six Flags in St. Louis for their "end of the school year hurrah." We decided to leave Caleb with Nana. On our way home we got a call, I could hear him screaming in the background. The seizures were coming continually. Nana loaded him up and we drove like mad people to get to our house. Chad got him out of the car, handed him to me and he went into a frontal lobe seizure.

These things are scary, they don't look like a "typical" seizure. They are hard to diagnose, supposedly. But I was certain that what I was looking at was a frontal lobe seizure. He stared off, looked up to the right and then screamed and flailed on the couch, bicycled his legs and lost control of his bladder. He jumped out of my arms and ran straight into the wall screaming. I picked him up, he looked as though he was in severe pain. This from a child who could be bleeding profusely and only be concerned if you were going to have to hold him down to get a band-aid on him. It was so hard to watch, and I couldn't imagine how hard it was on him to have to experience them.

He also began having seizures in his sleep, typically myoclonic seizures that are just brief intense jerks or partial seizures which would involve rhythmic shaking. At this point, Caleb slept with me, every night. I was concerned that he would go into Status Epilepticus (uncontrolled seizures despite intervention). We weaned him off Depakote, which was thought to be causing tremors and off of the Keppra. They added Clonezapam to his regimen. He was so tired all of the time, but could not relax, he was still terrified to go to sleep. With all the changes in medication we hoped for improvement, but he seemed to just worsen continually.

He had another round of these back to back frontal lobe seizures at church one night. He was a basket case, scared, screaming, pulling at his lips, flailing, jumping, falling, it was awful. I put him in the car to get him home and gave him some extra clonezapam, this time it seemed to help them slow and I was so grateful. For once the new medication was showing results, we were so hopeful.

Working for a few months and then failing seemed to become the trend with anticonvulsants in Caleb's treatment.

We took him back to Louisville in June and had another EEG ran. We needed him to seize on EEG. This would be the only way to get a good picture of what was truly going on. I had watched Caleb have a seizure while watching Cinderella before. So, we put the DVD on to hopefully see if this would occur again. He tremored and the EEG did not show a seizure but "epileptic activity" on the left side. At least that was something. Another seizure was caught later that night during Caleb's sleep. Caleb was sent home on only the Clonezapam, and I was worried. Rightfully so.

On June 16th Caleb experienced back to back seizures. We were at

Nana and Papa's and to "verify" what we were dealing with, one of the Neurology nurses asked us to video what we were seeing to "prove" if these were seizures or behavior. I was so mad at her questioning us. But we took video of the seizures. It was heartbreaking. He screamed, he said "it's going again" over and over. They were 2 minutes apart like clockwork. The DiaStat helped to calm them, but it was just heartbreaking that this sweet boy who was almost non-verbal was trying to tell us he was seizing. He hurt, he wanted comfort, and all I could do was hold him. It was enough to make all of us in the family just sick to have to see, and there we all were, helpless.

On the 29th after viewing the video, the Neurologist at Louisville agreed with my diagnosis and added Zonegran to his regimen. Caleb was physically exhausted. His sleep was constantly disrupted. And there was little to no talking at all. It was just not going well …and July would bring us worse.

Just like the year before July 4th was a bad, bad day. Caleb had back to back seizures. I had ran out of DiaStat at home, so we called an ambulance to take him to the local hospital. It took them an hour to go down to the pharmacy and get DiaStat for us. Meanwhile he seized uncontrollably. I promised Caleb then, never again would that happen. I made sure I always had back up medication for break through seizures, or Status Epilepticus from that point on.

This seizure episode was clearly a Status Epilepticus event. Looking back I was livid that the hospital staff did not respond as they should have. They wanted to do procedures, blood draws, CAT scans, I told them NO, I need DiaStat NOW! It still took 15 minutes after that point, but some nurse took mercy on us and went to the pharmacy herself to get it. I still get upset thinking about how upset he was, how exhausted he was and how it took an hour to get medication. Bless his sweet little heart, from that day on there were multiple DiaStat kits in this house.

We increased his Zonegran dosage, but the seizures continued. To try to help him be calm and relax so he could nap we took him to Aunt Ellen's one day and let him ride on the lawnmower with her. Since he was very little he liked to ride on the lawnmower with Papa or Chad or anyone. He liked riding period. So, when he could relax it was a blessing, and whenever we could we worked in some lawnmower time for him!

We added Prednisone to try and see if it would help at all with speech and possibly with the seizures too. We were doing summer school through Extended School Year services at Hendron/ Lone Oak. One day at school he said "Mickey Mouse," and while working on fine-motor skills, "Try it again." We were so encouraged, and cautiously, I was hoping that the steroids were making a difference.

Chapter 5: Losing Skills But Finding Hope

In mid-July Caleb contracted a red throat and we had to start an antibiotic for that, which was likely the cause of increased seizure activity earlier in the month. He was just a mess, he would wring his hands or play with wheels on his trucks continually. He was not "with us". My heart was breaking again. We were loosing skills that he had once had by the day. And the seizures were not relenting.

The thought from Louisville was that the nervousness was coming from the steroids, so we increased his Clonezapam dosage to counter that.

We went to visit some family in Birmingham for a few days. He said "Swimming in the pool" and "Take me in" when we got to the hotel one evening. Caleb loved the pool, he loved water. I was so glad he was excited to be able to go swimming and to be able to make that connection to talk about it to us, it was a blessing, just a few words, but so wonderful. We were prayerful that somehow he could find those connections more frequently.

He had an accident in Birmingham too, just as we had got into the hotel room one night. Caleb bounced on a chair and fell completely forward onto the edge of the end table. Looking back, it was quite possible that he had seized and lost his balance. He hit his forehead, right between his eyes was split open and I ran to the bathroom with him. Ellen was there and called Nana and Papa who had just left our room, to come back. We were trying to stop the bleeding but it wasn't slowing. I could feel my loss of adrenaline, but we had to get through this. Nana helped me hold Caleb and do cold compresses. Ellen jumped in the car and found the nearest drugstore and got some liquid band-aid. Papa came in to help hold him and Nana, Ellen and I somehow managed to "glue" his skin back together. Nana had a butterfly band-aid and we used that to seal it. We kept him awake for about ½ an hour to make sure he didn't have a concussion. I remember the relief when the whole ordeal was over. We evidently did a good job, there was very little of a scar once it healed….clearly we could do a commercial for liquid band-aid!

Caleb's nervous repetitive behavior of wringing his hands had now moved to rotating wheels on cars all day. The seizures were still present. And his words were there some, but overall they were less in number and consistency. So the prednisone was weaned.

During these days we were going weeks at time without being able to break through to coerce a smile. But one morning watching Bear in the Blue House do the "Cha Cha Cha", he smiled and it made my day! Video favorites like Bear in the Blue House and Barney seemed to be the only thing that would calm him at times, and the routine of watching his favorite episodes over and over was something that we would try not to do….but at times were inevitable. There is a Barney song for every thing you'll ever deal with in life. And I know that Caleb learned his colors from him, and that he was special. One day, while he could still speak some, Caleb sang part of the "Everyone is Special" song to me, saying "you are special, special" over and over. It was precious, and I sang the whole song to him, he smiled at me and went back to playing with his truck. I could kiss that purple dinosaur for giving me that moment with him!

Realizing that we were going to be dealing with medical personnel on a regular basis, I wrote social stories for Caleb about hooking him up to an EEG, I had a lead wire for him to look at and hold. I took pictures of hospital beds, rooms, needles, nurses and doctors everywhere with us. The "Emergency Bag" held all of his hospital cards, a "NO NO" or Velcro arm splint to cover his IV, and all of his extra medications. It went everywhere he went from that day on.

By August, we were losing him. The seizures were taking their toll. Everything was slowing, speech, cognition, even his bowels had slowed down to the point I had to do an enema to help him with chronic constipation. The plan was to put him on Lamictal, a good drug for generalized seizures and wean him off the Zonegran. His constant need for turning wheels had moved to his hands wringing together and now he was moving his hands to his mouth constantly. He would not make eye contact with us at all, and his words were gone, he would just grunt at us sometimes. Although, one afternoon right after a partial seizure he sat on his swing and said what sounded like "swing me" to me. It's amazing how something so debilitating like chronic seizures can just ignite a part of your brain and for a moment, what you couldn't connect is back, for just an instant.

It was time for Caleb to start Kindergarten. I was reluctant at sending him at all. But, it gave him a chance to interact with someone besides me all the time, and he seemed to deal with being in this new environment as well as possible. He had great teachers who loved him, and I was pleased to have them on our team.

I spoke with an Educational Consultant, Marsha Harper, who had become a dear friend to us and had helped with Caleb's educational planning since preschool days. When she came to see Caleb in Kindergarten, she cried with me when she saw how much he had regressed. She told me these words, and they carried me through some of those rough days that I unknowingly would have to come "Meet him where he is, wherever that is, every day." I decided right then, that it was no longer about stressing over educating Caleb, but about keeping him healthy at all cost. It was also about finding a way to get those smiles back, and reconnecting with our sweet boy.

September brought us a few more smiles, and Caleb laughed when we tickled him sometimes. Those seem like very little things, but to us they were monumental moments. I recall him walking into school one day without falling, and that was a huge little moment too. He was very tired and we started seeing more Myoclonic seizures. These are just brief jerks that look like what you do when you feel like you're falling when you go to sleep and your body jerks….only he would have them constantly when trying to go to sleep and during awake periods of the day. He walked all day with his head upside down one day at school, I know his head just had to ache. This continued for about a week, and I was greatly concerned that he was experiencing another change in activity.

We were prayerful that somehow weaning Zonegran and increasing Lamictal would be just the thing. It was hard to see him regress so much, for Chad and I, but also for the girls. Peyton especially had questions about "is he ever going to get better?" and all we could say is that we were hoping so, and that we needed to keep praying that he could get better.

October of '07, we were increasing the Lamictal slowly, and were up to 25mg am and pm, but the seizures were still breaking through. Caleb had contracted a bad cold and threw up some flem at school. It was my birthday, Oct. 15th, so I picked him up early from school that day and went to Wal-mart to get some juice for him. He had a full blown Tonic seizure, right there in the cart. This is what most people refer to as a "grand-mal" seizure. His eyes rolled back in his head, his chin dropped to his chest, his arms raised above his head rigidly, his legs were stiff and out-stretched. I got out of there as quick as possible, got him to the car and gave him extra Clonezapam (which we were using for breakthrough seizures only at the time). He slept.

An upper respiratory, sinus and gastrointestinal infection were found the next day by the pediatrician, and Caleb was put on a round of antibiotics. He also had a red throat, and I was having a tough time getting him to eat anything.

By the end of October, Caleb had lost about 9 lbs. and was constipated all the time. I had started some pro-biotics for him that were helping some. But with all the weight loss I was concerned.

We went to Louisville and met with the nurse who recommended a weight gaining diet with high fat/ high calories. I asked to put Caleb on the Ketogenic Diet, but was told that parents don't stick with it and they just didn't do that there. I was completely disappointed. It was the only thing out there that I thought could possibly help his seizures, and the staff there wouldn't consider it. It was disheartening to say the least.

After a patient has been on 2 antiepileptic medications and they are not successful at seizure control, the chances of ever gaining seizure control drop off dramatically. We had already been on 7 in a little over a year and were making no gains. I questioned what else could be done. The nurse did tell me about a Vegas Nerve Stimulator that is basically a "defribulator" for the brain. She said the earliest we could get an appointment to meet with the one doctor that did that procedure would be April or May of '08. I was not impressed.

November brought his 6th birthday, and he did not feel well at all, he was very tired, had a runny nose and cough and would not eat well. He experienced more tonic seizure activity, but because of the illness we didn't change his medication. He was on antibiotics and we were trying to get him over that so the seizures would slow, but it just wasn't working quickly enough.

We still were working hard with him daily, and some days we would have really good days, he might make good eye contact with you (which would usually bring us all to tears!) or he might be able to make a choice, every little thing, every baby step forward was a tremendous success!

Over the fall, it had become apparent to us and to his new school team at Hendron Lone Oak Elementary that Caleb's legs were just not as strong, he could still stand and walk some, but his stamina was diminishing to the point that by the end of November his teachers would have to carry him when they left the classroom. We were doing the same at home, he would not walk outside of our house, he just wore out too quickly. We had bought a jogging stroller earlier in the year, because typical strollers just weren't big enough for him. But I realized that we were moving to the point where a wheelchair might be where we were headed. I searched online and found one I thought might work, so the battle with insurance began and we waited.

Being on Lamictal was helping Caleb to be more "present" with us at times, one December morning he brought me a book "Giggle, Giggle, Quack" which was one of his favorites and he let me read the whole thing to him. It was a day, just like any other, but made special by his ability to make a connection. I learned to let a moment like that carry a positive hope for a long time.

Seizures began changing again for Caleb and Gelastic or "laughing" seizures came into play. They look like a belly rolling laugh, but then they become different. Seeing these from a child who rarely grins, at first we hoped were him responding. But they are not provoked, and come out of nowhere, and he could not stop. They are seizures nonetheless, and it crushed our hearts.

He also experienced tonic, partial and absence seizures that month, so another call was made to Louisville. At this point they opted to do another EEG, but I really wanted them to do another MRI just in case we were dealing with a tumor. Gelastic seizures stem from the Hippocampus, as it controls emotion. They would not do the MRI, but said that based on his EEG they would recommend the Vegas Nerve Stimulator, but the consult appointment couldn't be scheduled until May 2008.

The neat thing about learning about the VNS was that there was a magnet that you could "wand" over the implant that would make it fire and hopefully stop a seizure. Just a week before learning about this, Camille (who loved Tinkerbell), came up to me and said, "Mama, Caleb just needs a magic wand, we could use it and "poof" his seizure would be gone." It was simply amazing that they were telling us that just such a thing did exist. Our hope was that someone could get it implanted in him soon so the chance of something working against these relentless seizures could begin.

More tonic seizures increased by the end of the month. He was having trouble again with swallowing after these seizures. I called the nurse at Louisville again after the first of January, Caleb was literally climbing the walls to get away from the seizures, she said "you may just need to get a psych consult". This ended our relationship with Louisville. I could not believe after all our sweet boy had been through that this was her "help".

Chapter 6: Finding Kindred Spirits

I talked to our Pediatrician, Dr. Mudd and he agreed with me that taking him somewhere else might be the best choice. He had a patient who had seen a Dr. Gregory Barnes at Vanderbilt Children's Hospital in Nashville. So, I asked him to refer us and set up an appointment. We had one set for January 15th to meet Dr. Barnes.

I was relieved to have an appointment with Vanderbilt, we just had to make it until then. However, Caleb's seizures were increasing again. Concerned he might be ill again, I took him to Dr. Mudd. I talked with him about the increase in tonic seizure activity and he was concerned with me. He advised us to take him to Vanderbilt Children's ER. So Chad and I loaded him up and we left with anxious but hopeful hearts.

January 9th, 2008, the first doctor to walk into our ER room was a young man. His name was Dr. Rob Carson. He and the Neurology team had already reviewed Caleb's information. He walked in and took notes over my "history of Caleb's seizures". He was kind, he was interested, he was compassionate. I was so thankful. He also said he worked with Dr. Barnes, so I knew that everything that was discussed would be handed to our new doctor to view. One thing that Dr. Carson mentioned right away was the Modified Atkins or Ketogenic Diet for seizure control. I was so relieved, he spoke my language! I had been trying since August to research and get information and had been completely dismissed at Louisville when trying to discuss it. I was so thankful that this was now an option.

We were admitted and Caleb had another EEG ran. We saw the attending Neurologist, who was so kind and came up with a plan to increase the Lamictal drastically to try to help with control.
He also mentioned a surgeon there who could do a VNS implant.

Then we met with Mary Montgomery, a dietician who works with pediatric epilepsy. She was wonderful and so kind to us. She said we'd get started on the diet while in the hospital, I was so glad! Finally, someone who was willing to try something to help us!!

We had Caleb on a Gluten Free/Casein Free/Yeast Free diet which he'd been on for 3 years at this point. So we did a Modified Atkins/GF/CF/Yeast free diet for him. It was tough. He was limited to 10 grams of carbohydrates daily. This is equal to the amount of carbs in ½ of a medium sized apple. He could not have sugar in anything, no juice, not in his medications, not on his body. The kind of lotions and even his toothpaste could have "hidden carbs" that would send his body out of Ketosis.

The Ketogenic diet or a modified Atkins diet is started in children/adults with epilepsy to try to mimic starvation. In the Bible Jesus refers to a type of epileptic person whose seizures could only be controlled by "prayer and fasting" Matthew 17:21. This concept was developed into the ketogenic diet by researchers at Johns Hopkins University in the 1920's. The diet is high fat and low carbohydrate. It is recommended to be started in a medical facility so that education for the family can begin while the patient is safely started on the diet. When fats are broken down a byproduct of that are ketones. The actual mechanism of how this works remains unknown. But many with seizures have become seizure free using this diet. Even more have had a reduction in their seizure numbers by using the diet.

For us, for Caleb, it was worth the hard effort to get this started. It could make all the difference, and he deserved the very best we could give him.

On January 15th, 2008, we met Dr. Gregory Barnes for the first time. It was a blessing. He was the first person to say "options" and "plan" to us. The plan was to continue on the diet, continue on Lamictal and Clonezapam which he agreed weren't really working well but were "keeping us out of the ER" for now. We would be scheduled for a 4 day EEG and an MRI. The possibilities were that we were dealing with a type of seizure syndrome called Lennox-Gastaut, or that he was having left temporal lobe focus seizures that could be dealt with in a surgical procedure called a corpus colostomy, and then there was the possibility of the VNS. So, we were thankful for options. Dr. Barnes was so kind to us and to Caleb, we could tell right away that his compassion for these children was great.

On the home front the daunting task of getting Caleb to take all of his medications grinded up and made into a paste for him to take was no fun. I would save his juice box, which now contained water sweetened with stevia (a sugar replacement) and reward him with it when he got the meds down. Bless his heart, it was just no good. But, he'd done it before when we were on Depakote sprinkles and had to mix it in applesauce, and deep down I think he knew that we were trying to help him. I was also getting good at weighing out all his foods and cooking mountains of bacon for him. We fed him ALL DAY. It was a huge deal to get all these fattening foods into this tiny little guy in a 24 hour period. But he did it, and it seemed to get easier. HE LOVED BACON, so that part was always the easiest. When I would start the microwave he knew I was warming up his bacon for him and he would come and stand and wait for it. He was so precious. His big brown eyes and a little grin was all it took to melt my heart. Being able to feed him what he liked was the easy part, but keeping him from eating mountains of his favorite "Puffcorn" was tough. It's like airy popcorn and he could eat an entire bag of it in one setting. But with the carb limit I could give him ½ a cup as a treat. As always, Caleb learned to accept this new change without any major meltdown. I knew he wanted more, but we just brought in pepperoni after that if he wanted something else. He loved pepperoni too, and that was allowed in mass quantity on the diet!

The stress from everything Caleb was going through, was carrying over to me and on January 22nd I went into Addison's Crisis. Luckily, the ER doctor at the local hospital was able to get the necessary steroid replacement in me that I needed. I had woke during the night vomiting. Chad left for work, thinking I just had a virus and I assured him I thought I was okay. By 6 I had called for recruits to get the kids ready for school, which included cooking Caleb's food for breakfast and packing 2 snacks and lunch for him. Plus, getting the girls ready and to school. Everyone left to deliver the kids and told me they'd be right back. When they got back I had vomited more and gone into shock. They called an ambulance and by the time they got me there I was blue around the mouth and my extremities. After several attempts they were able to get a line in to start the necessary meds. They stabilized me in CCU and then moved me to the floor, and I did fine. I contacted my Endocrinologist in Nashville and he advised me of my "stress dosing" procedure that I should do and scheduled a follow up. Nothing like a little drama to go with everything else in our lives, but it was a wake up call to me that I had to be certain and take care of me so I could take care of Caleb.

During my hospitalization Caleb had dropped out of Ketosis although everyone had done a wonderful job sticking to the diet. However, he had been drinking lots of fluids, so we started restricting them to try to help his ketones to increase again. His seizure activity was also increasing again. So this was not good.

But a bit of good news in the midst of some tough days, we were finally approved for a wheelchair and we put in the order. That was a huge blessing!

Meanwhile, January seemed not to want to let go of us and Caleb contracted a virus that sent his seizures into warp speed. We made another ER trip to Vandy and Caleb was placed on Felbatol. This is a "last resort" kind of drug, but has helped numerous people with epilepsy. His blood levels of the drug would have to be checked regularly, but the Lamictal and Clonezapam were running out of power against Caleb's seizures. I felt like every time we found something that would help a little, Caleb's beautifully made brain would find a way to go back to "normal for him" which was to seize. It was so frustrating, but again we were hopeful.

I also talked to the Neurologists that were in the ER about Caleb's seizures causing him to fall and they recommended a helmet. Caleb was always a "head sensitive" child, but he liked deep pressure, so I was hoping that this helmet would somehow just feel like a big hug to him….and he adapted, brilliantly, as always.

I cannot explain how hard that ER visit was. I had to sign papers that said I wouldn't sue if my child died from taking these medications, but in that same moment prayed that this would stop his seizures. I had to come to grips with the fact that Caleb may never be without seizures. That was tough to swallow. But the hope of tests to come and a VNS or a possible surgical "fix" were out there, so we trudged on.

We are so blessed to have such a strong family who pulled together to help us through these rough patches, and we had an extended family and church family and a support team on Caringbridge.org . All of our family were able to keep in touch, and we were so thankful to be able to have this resource to keep everyone updated about Caleb's ever changing health.

February 6, 2008 , was Caleb's last day at school. I received a call, and Caleb's seizures were clustering. He was in Status Epilepticus. I instructed his teacher to give him DiaStat (rectal valium) and I jumped in the car to get to him. He was listless, and exhausted. His teachers were in tears, as was I. But the ambulance was waiting and I left with him in my arms in route to the hospital. Vanderbilt was called and they wanted him in the ER there as soon as possible. So rather than wait for the long time of transport, we opted to take him ourselves. Supposedly a video-EEG room was open, but in the 3 hours it took us to get there, that room was gone. We were moved to an observation room. Caleb was seizing constantly. He was hitting at us in fear, then he would seize, then he would lose bowel control, we'd clean him up and it would start all over. It was the worst night I could imagine. Ellen was with me and she called it a "horror film". That night, those seizures and the look of fear and our inability, even after 2 rounds of Ativan to stop them was just overwhelming. Finally a round of IV Valium seemed to slow them down…for the moment.

The seizures were unrelenting and for the next 9 days we would watch him cycle seizures, endlessly, some occurred during awake periods, however, the cycling of seizures would start about 10 minutes after he went to sleep, it was like clockwork. We were helpless, and he was not responding to Valium that was moved to a regular regimen for him. We did get the MRI done during this stay, which was an answered prayer. And during this hospital stay we met some really great neurologists, but we were met with some really tough facts:

1. Caleb's new cycling of seizures at sleep could be a new normal for him.
2. Caleb's EEG reflected that he most likely did not have any "epilepsy syndrome".
3. Caleb was born with a brain malformation that happened in-utero called Bifrontal Cortical Dysplasia.

4. Caleb's neurons in his brain did not connect to the cerebral cortex.
5. Caleb's history of learning and then regressing was symptomatic of the physical abnormality.
6. The seizures that we were seeing and marking, they were all seizures, every time, and there were some that we did not see.

Dr. Barnes came in and said that he didn't know how but we got on the books for a Positron Emission Tomography (PET) scan on the 29th, I told him we had a lot of people praying, and he smiled. He sent us home on 4 anticonvulsants (Depakote, Felbatol, Lamictal and Tranxene) and a new emergency plan if things got worse. I was to update him by email weekly. It was a tough stay, but we were hoping that the PET scan would show an area that was truly the problem and that it could be removed. However, he said that it was looking like it was inoperable. It is sad to say you are praying for brain surgery, but we were praying for just that. It could potentially "fix" the problem, we were hoping.

Meanwhile, the seizures were coming so frequently that we physically had to be at Caleb's side at all times. This was a tough job, but we managed. Chad was home at night to help and the weekends, and even the girls were pitching in and sitting with him for a moment while we got meds or food ready for him. The girls were starting to recognize his seizures as well. This was tough as a mom, to know that your other children were being educated to the point of being able to recognize seizures right along with me…it also meant that Caleb was having lots of seizures.

We were doing weekly blood draws, daily ketone checks, and had moved to an even more strict version of the Ketogenic diet to try to bump up his numbers.

Here is what he ate on a daily basis to try to keep him in ketosis:

Breakfast: 1 fried egg, 15 pieces bacon, 1 piece sausage
Lunch: 3oz. Of beef brisket
Supper: 6 grilled shrimp and 3 oz. of pork chop
Snacks: 68 pepperoni slices, 4 oz. strawberries, 1 cup of puff corn
Drinks: 12 - 4oz, cups of water with stevia flavoring

It wasn't the most pleasant menu, but even doing all this Caleb was going out of Ketosis if he didn't eat every bite of every thing. His intake had to be specific.

At first when we started the Modified Atkins/Keto diet, we did see some seizure reduction. However, it seemed to fade in effectiveness, just as the mulitple anticonvulsants seemed to.

We waited with anxiousness for the PET Scan. We tried to keep up the daily schedule at home with one on one therapists, homebound schooling, occupational therapists, all that in between the medication regimen and seizures were enough to consume the day. But, Caleb was not doing any better.

 He would stand at the front door and hit it and moan until someone took him out for a ride in the car. So needless to say, many hours started being spent driving Caleb around. Gas was at an all time high, so I would call Chad and tell him to work overtime, that Ellen and I and Zeb had been driving Caleb all day. It truly was the only thing that calmed him. We would put him in and go. Eventually he would start seizing, and Ellen would drive and I would sit with him and monitor them and count.

 The seizure log was getting pretty thick, and I realized I needed a new notebook to chart in. Caleb was having around 60 seizures a day at the time. Several of them being tonic seizures. When he had them while awake it looked like a "cross formation," it was horrifying. His entire body would stiffen, his eyes roll back , his head would flex downward, his arms would rise up. Someone had to be right there to catch him or he'd just plummet to the floor. It was scary. I was waiting on the helmet we were advised to order to get here, and it just couldn't get here fast enough.

Finally PET day came. Our favorite EEG tech, Alisha Morgan, came over to the adult hospital (where the procedure would have to be done) and hooked him up in record time. Caleb was very tired, but we didn't notice any visible seizures while he was on the EEG, but in 30 minutes he was taken off and they took him in for the PET. He did fine and came out tired but resting well. His seizures started back up by 5 pm. We were so glad to have it over with, but now the real agony of waiting for the answer came.

Our church family at Maple Hill Church of Christ, they prayed for us continually. They also sent a huge basket of Caleb's favorite: CARS!! As well, sweet cards and gifts of encouragement for us and the girls too. It was so uplifting to have a great support from them.

We also were growing in numbers of Team Caleb members on our Caringbridge site. Many would sign our "Guestbook" and it would just make our day to see encouragement coming from people literally around the world!

Caleb's days were seeming to become filled with him seizing, being nervous, unhappy, unsettled, all day long. It was exhausting just to watch him suffer, and agonizing that we were doing all we could and this was "the best" we could achieve for him. Helpless doesn't seem to cover the feeling, but that is how I felt. I could not imagine how he felt. Did he know that we were trying all we could? Did he understand that the doctors were doing all they could?

One Sunday I loaded him up and tried to take him to Nana and Papa's to be with the family. They were at worship. At this point Caleb's health did not allow him to be around many people. I shielded him from germs and public places. As soon as I got him out and unloaded at their house he went to the door and hit it and whined. I loaded him back up and left, I realized that he was trying to tell me that he wanted to be home. That was where, at least sometimes, he could be content. It broke my heart, I cried all the way home, for him. How sad it must have been for him to not feel comfortable anywhere, for him to feel anxious and scared and restless. My heart hurt for him, I just wanted him to be happy.

Monday, March 3rd, 2008--

The PET Scan results were in, and the worst possibility had come to fruition. Caleb's PET scan showed diffuse bilateral cortical dysplasia. In short, there were areas across both of his frontal lobes so taking out ½ of his brain would only leave him with another "bad ½" that would still continue to cause seizures. So in short, surgery was not an option. This was devastating news. We were just sick.

Chapter 7: The Home Front

We were not giving up. There was no way to treat the actual problem, so now we were just going to see if there was any way we could reduce the symptoms- specifically, the seizures. There were some options still out there, and I was determined we were going to explore all we could. In the same turn, we were realizing that this could be something that would worsen, but we would make the best of it and be thankful for wherever he was - because he was with us. The difficulties of our day were minimal in comparison to what our sweet Caleb was having to deal with. And yet, he was brave and loving and patient, through all of this turmoil. If he was going to have to live this- I was going to carry him, and there was an army of good people surrounding us.

The tough days did wear on me, Chad took most of the blows, as all good husbands should…but it was tough for our marriage and our family. The girls still needed individual attention. Ellen was spending every day at our house helping me with Caleb, and Zeb needed her individual attention too. But, then again, when the tough days got tougher, I would look up and there would be Peyton and Camille, waiting to help with whatever it was that was needed to help their sweet Bubba. Zeb was so good to Caleb too, he was the "little brother" that took the blows sometimes… but also, was a great "protector". Zeb would go with us for the blood draws weekly. He stood right next to Caleb's wheelchair, and would watch the nurses like a hawk. He would watch them draw the blood, and when it was all over, he would give Caleb a pat, hold onto his chair, and walk him out. He got the nickname

"Bodyguard" from the nurses!

Days of long drives continued, we would start sometimes at 8 and drive around until lunch, drop by the house for literally a moment and head back out. Sometimes we drove up to 8 hours in a day. Caleb's seizure counts continued to rise.

We spoke with Dr. Barnes about his continual increase, and the decision was to increase his Felbatol and stop the Lamictal. He was still on Tranxene and Depakote as well. So we were hopeful the increase in Felbatol would help. However, his platelets began dropping. Now we were concerned that the Aplastic Anemia was occurring. I did some research and found that sometimes with a dose increase, platelets might temporarily decrease, but that they should rebound. So we started praying that they would increase, and little by little, they did improve. He was also having some low glucose levels at this time as well, so we were watching blood work numbers for any changes faithfully.

March brought some nice weather and we did get to put in some miles of walking rather than driving. So volunteers would come to the house and take Caleb for walks around the block in his wheelchair. His helmet finally had arrived, and as usual, Caleb adapted to it without any problems…just getting it on him while he was moving around was the challenge!

There were gas cards and goodie bags sent to us on a weekly basis from friends, teachers, and family. And the name "TEAM CALEB" was used to describe all of those who were helping with his daily care.

There are no words to describe how thankful we were as well, to have members of Team Caleb at Vanderbilt. Dr. Barnes met with us on March 18th, to discuss fully the PET and to answer all of my questions. I am a mom with a "Google MD", I research everything. So, when diffuse bilateral cortical dysplasia was the diagnosis, try the web search for that one… there is very little, because it is rare. What I did find were excerpts from scientific research, research papers, and filled with medical jargon. So I would research until I could figure it out. And from what I could find, the worst was possible, so I needed to hear this from a Neurologist. So I asked the tough questions. Dr. Barnes gave me the truth. I asked him about prognosis, and he said "In cases like this, with Caleb's situation, I feel very fortunate if we can get them to 18, I feel very lucky if they are here past 18." His voice trembled a bit and he continued, "that is why when you call me, email me, I hang on your every word. I analyze everything you say and feel about your son. There is no room for errors at this point and I understand that." I knew he hurt for us, but that he was willing to do everything he could to help us keep Caleb with us as long as possible.

So we drove home, with heavy hearts, but with hopeful hearts. Knowing Caleb's lifespan would undoubtedly be shorter than we wished, but hoping we could provide a quality of life for him that would allow happiness and somewhat stable health. It was hard to deal with, the drive home, Chad and I and Ellen all had "meltdowns". And when we got home, our house was full of family. We sent the kids to play and shared the tough news. It was hard. But we were determined to push on for this brave little boy, who still managed to smile from time to time, and who had stolen all of our hearts with his eyes.

The seizures by the end of the month were climbing upward, and Caleb was waking in the early morning hours. He would wake at 2 and be a nervous wreck until finally a huge tonic would finally break through and then myoclonic seizures would follow.

One morning he'd already had 90 seizures before we even got out of the bed.

I researched more, and found more I didn't want to know. I discovered that SUDEP (Sudden Unexplained Death in Epilepsy Patients) in children with bilateral cortical dysplasia was a possibility. This cut to my heart, and I tried not to focus on that. I had to hope, and pray, and monitor everything that Caleb had going on daily so I could keep Dr. Barnes informed and this would enable him to make the best possible decisions for Caleb's treatment.

March 26th, 2008--
Caleb developed a possible sinus infection which led to a status epilepticus event. At 3 am he had an 8 minute long seizure and clustered into repetitive partial seizures. I gave him DiaStat (rectal valium) and called the ambulance. He was transported to the local hospital. Then he was moved to Vanderbilt Children's via ambulance after spiking a 105.2 temp and beginning to vomit. He

received a load of Dilantin to stop the seizures, but after he spiked the temperature he had finally slowed. Caleb was not like most kids, sometimes a spike in temperature actually improved his seizure activity.

(My theory on this is: If your "normal" is seizing and your brain is "inflamed" then when you run a temperature that is your body's way of fighting infection and inflammation. So naturally, for a kid with a brain malformation, this kind of allowed his brain to "quiet". It's completely not proven, but it made sense to me, and someday maybe they can develop a medication to mimic the process that a fever naturally has so that this concept could reduce seizure activity….if anyone ever markets this, you owe me royalties!)

He was moved to Vandy, and admitted. Neurology worked hard to come up with a new plan to "put out the fire". Meanwhile, we fought getting seizure medications into him while he struggled with chronic vomiting. All tests came back negative for viral infections, pneumonia, respiratory illness, etc. The thought was that he could be suffering from encephalitis (infection of the brain). Rather than put his body through an onslaught of tests, they gave him a shot of Rocephin, which would fight off any infection. It was more important to treat him and see if it would work than to put him through more pain, and for that measure of comfort for him, I was grateful. It did work, and he improved with the help of some Zofran. But in the end, they felt that all of this was brought on by the seizure activity.

We went home and the seizures continued, but a Felbatol increase finally brought numbers down from 100+ a day down to a minimum of 30 and highs in the 80's. But any reduction was good.

We were heading for a Vegas Nerve Stimulator (VNS). Although it was helpful to many in up to a 50% reduction in seizures, we were hoping for any improvement. Dr . Barnes met with us and discussed the new plans. We would try to keep Caleb out of the ER by adding Gabitril, and to get the VNS in. And realistically we knew that this would be just like any other medication we'd been on. There would likely be a period of improvement, and after increasing it to it's fullest potential or "maximum dosage", then it would lose it's effectiveness. However, as a parent, there is always that glimmer of hope, that need for something to work that consumes your heart and overflows and flushes reality out. So, although I knew the statistics, I was hopeful.

Seizures continued to climb over 200 a day, then to 350, so then when we saw a day with 100 seizures, we became grateful. Sad.

The driving continued. Nana, Uncle John and a dear friend Susie, took shifts when Aunt Ellen couldn't help. We increased Tranxene further to try to help with seizure control. On nice days, we would walk him around the neighborhood for hours. Two of his teachers, Mrs. Kim, and Ms. Deena would come to work with him, and really they helped us by giving us a break. They would walk him around the block or read to him or just hold him while he watched Barney if he was content enough to be in the house.

Ellen used the verse Psalms 55:22 several times on our Caringbridge page. It says "Cast you burden upon the Lord, and he shall sustain you." I know many nights while counting seizures all I could do was pray. And at some point during this time I realized that I had moved past the prayers for healing and faced that I needed to pray for strength for me and comfort for Caleb.

One day we thought he was trying to say "hey" to us, whether he was or not, we said he did, because we wanted so badly to hear him speak again.

We spent most of May 2008 on eggshells. Counting up to 500 seizures a day. Adjusting medications. Anxiously awaiting the VNS implant, and hoping that after getting it in that it would work. Caleb had a moment of happiness early one morning while running in for juice when he eyed the Bob the Builder ride at Wal-mart. We put him on and we got lots of pictures of him smiling, it was precious.

We started with Home Health and they were hopefully going to set up coming to our house to do blood work so we wouldn't have to go to the flu/germ filled hospital to get it done weekly. I took him to the park one nice day and realized that he couldn't even stand long enough to balance himself for me to get him down the slide. So I carried him, and slid down with him and when we left, I cried. He was loosing his legs and his freedom day by day. But, when he went down the slide, he smiled, and I told myself to "buck up" and just be happy that he found some kind of happiness in that.

A friend of a friend heard about Caleb and all of the driving we were doing. He brought us his golf cart to drive Caleb around the neighborhood. What a blessing that was! It was a joy and he enjoyed it so much! We were averaging around 200 seizures daily, but we were trying our best to find opportunities for Caleb to enjoy himself and provide some family time together. The girls enjoyed riding the golf cart with us and that was something they could truly do "with him" so it was just great.

We worked in a visit to the zoo in Nashville one day, Caleb enjoyed being strolled for hours anywhere, and although he seldom would look at the animals, the girls could enjoy it "with him" and he was happy as a lark as long as we were moving!

Caleb was honored at Field Day at his old school, Hendron Lone Oak Elementary. He was feeling well enough that he got to ride with me and his teacher around the track on a convertible. They made t-shirts with his and two other students' names on them. All the children waved and clapped for him as we drove around the football field, of course I cried. It was amazing. They gave us part of the proceeds from the shirts they made to help with expenses, we were just overwhelmed. To know so many cared for us and loved Caleb meant the world. I was so proud of Caleb that day, to know he touched the lives of those children and taught them to care for those that are weaker than they are. He was like a celebrity, and I just thought to myself, how wonderful these kids will be as grown ups because of moments like that, when they show kindness to those who aren't "just like them".

Chapter 8: Surgery, School and Sleeplessness

The date for the VNS implant was set. Dr. Matt Pearson would do the procedure on May 27th, 2008. We all wore our "TEAM CALEB" T-shirts Ellen and Susie had made. Many people from Texas to Connecticut to Georgia and beyond were wearing their shirts in support of us that day. The Vandy staff thought they were awesome, we did too! The surgery lasted 1 ½ hours. A pocket was made in the tissue above his heart and the stimulating device would be placed there. Then the wire leading to the Vegas Nerve which leads directly to the brain would carefully be wrapped around the nerve. Once the device was in, I learned to clean the area and what to look for if infection set in. Caleb was very sick from the anesthesia and vomited several times. We got Zofran running in him again so he would be able to take his medications, and luckily he was able to keep them down. We were discharged and scheduled to see Dr. Barnes in clinic to set the VNS.

Once it was in I can remember being afraid for Caleb, that he would feel the charge and that it would upset him. Dr. Barnes set it and he did have a reaction to it going off, but just got REALLY STILL like, "what was that" and then he was fine. I was OCD about when the silly thing was going off at first and I would write down the setting and the duration that it would fire and then how often it would fire and then I would write down the time it would fire so I would know if he did something reacting to it whether it was firing. Seriously, I don't know what I was thinking, but at the time I felt it was necessary, so I did it!
The seizures continued, around 300 daily. And we were nearing

another 4th of July, so I was anxious as usual.

We finally saw the magnet that comes with the VNS work to stop a long tonic seizure, so that was really exciting to think that I could stop a long tonic seizure. But soon that lost its effect.
While charting his seizures I noted that we did begin to see a larger reduction in his myoclonic seizure activity after a month of VNS therapy. So that was a blessing, we hoped it would last.

Caleb continued to lose his ability to stand, assist in any way in dressing, and would never be potty trained. We had accepted this, but many were asking us the "What are you going to do when" questions. Like, "How are you going to get him in the car when he weighs 100 lbs.?" or "When he gets bigger, what are you going to do about changing his diaper?" and to those questions I replied, "We will worry about it when we get there." And Ellen did too! We were too busy concentrating on getting through the day to even consider the what if's.

Changing a diaper in a bathroom for a small child can be an ordeal, but let me tell you, 3 people and a wheelchair in a handicapped stall is a bit of a stretch. One would hold him up while the other changed him as quick as possible. We would laugh at how crazy it would be every time, mostly to avoid crying, but nevertheless, I am sure the other people in the bathroom thought we had lost it!!

We were seeing Dr. Barnes every 4 weeks for VNS setting changes. As the 4th of July approached, Caleb's sleep was minimal at best and his tonic seizures were increasing in number and intensity. He always had his hands in his mouth at this point, and during tonic seizures many times I had to pry his hands out of his mouth to keep them from being clamped in. We increased his tranxene and kept him out of the ER on the 4th, so we were grateful.

Summer days were spent strolling the block with him in the wheelchair. His aide from school, Mrs. Tica started working for us and came to be with Caleb and help with him. It was a blessing to have extra hands.

We also saw Caleb sign "yes" to us when we gave him something he wanted. He hadn't done this in months, it was such a breakthrough that he was able to make that little connection. It didn't last long, but for the few days he could make that connection without interruption, we were so happy. It was him, communicating with us in a small way, but it was SO BIG!!

Constantly we were changing Caleb's medications, usually increasing them, to keep up with his ever increasing seizure activity. We had Dr. Barnes, and his trauma nurse, Ginny, who checked on us weekly, so we always felt safe and blessed that we could contact them for help at any time. We took a quick family summer trip with the family to Gatlinburg and Caleb enjoyed all the walking we did, he in his new wheelchair could just stroll for hours!! One morning, Chad and he were out for a walk down by the stream and met up with a mama bear and her two cubs! I was terrified when he came running back, Caleb's wheels were spinning! I think Caleb enjoyed the running his daddy was doing, not realizing they were in a bad location! So, we limited the walks to sidewalks and away from streams!

Caleb's tonic seizure activity continued to break through daily. Some days were worse than others, and I was seeing that "swiping" him with the magnetic wand for his VNS was no longer really successful at stopping his seizures every time. We started doing "maintenance swiping" to try to minimize Caleb's clustering of seizures. But, again, this seemed to slow his clustering temporarily, like for literally 5 minutes or so, and then he'd be right back at it.

By the end of the summer, we were seeing these large tonics increase in number and duration. Along with that, Caleb would have difficulty swallowing food. He was also having some episodes of wheezing. And to comfort himself he constantly had his hands in his mouth.

Caleb had begun to look like he just didn't feel well, all the time. It was difficult not to be upset about it, but if he had to deal with it, there was no room for complaint from me. The weather was hot, so once a day we were going for car rides to allow him to be "out of the house." However, he didn't seem to really enjoy these, but would just rest. Resting and being tired all day seemed to consume him. He didn't even want to spin the wheels on his trucks, so we knew something was up, but it was just difficult to put our finger on what that was.

Peyton, our oldest was starting 6th grade at Lone Oak Middle

School, and I was nervous for this change for her, but she did well, as always. Camille was starting 4th grade at Lone Oak Elementary, and was doing well. My girls are such hard workers at school. They were also very good to Caleb, and had learned lots of things that we never thought they would experience at their age. They could use sign language to speak to him, they used PECS cards to help him make choices, they were in tune to his sensory needs as well, and would always stop to give him a big "squeeze" if he needed it.

This was the beginning of another school year, but not a school year for Caleb. I was really sad that he would not be able to go. But truly, his health care and his daily schedule was so rigorous, there was no way for him to make it through a day at school.

I told my girls to be glad they could go to school, that they could tie their shoes, that they could talk to their friends, and choose their lunch. There would be new friends at school who had Autism or other developmental problems, and I told them to be kind to them and to help whenever they could. My girls are very sympathetic and loyal to children with special needs. If someone makes fun of a child with a disability, my girls will be the first to set them straight! If they see a teacher who doesn't know how to interact with a child with Autism or other disability, my girls will come home and tell me what that teacher did wrong and how they should have dealt with the problem. My girls are just amazing with kids with special needs because of their experiences with Caleb, and I know they will someday grow up to be awesome moms, teachers, doctors, etc.

So, Caleb and I began the year without school as our routine, and I grieved that loss. In the same turn I was so thankful to have a routine at home with my sweet little boy, all day. We still had Mrs. Tica, his aide to come and work with him and Ms. Deena, who had been one of his Pre-school aides started coming to help as well in the afternoons. We also had a new Homebound Teacher, Mrs. Sandy, who came to work with Caleb twice a week. With all of these extra hands in the afternoons, it was easier to get through the day with Caleb and make sure all his needs were met and then as soon as my help got there I would start on supper and get the girls doing their homework. Cooking became my "therapy."

August 6, 2008 -
Caleb began having episodes of labored breathing. Suspecting that this could have been an asthmatic episode, we took him to the doctor the next morning. Dr. Mudd checked him over, but there were no signs of infection and the episode had stopped on it's own. We did an x-ray just to be sure, but nothing was found. A week later Caleb went into Status Epilepticus, again. It was August 14th, and after administering DiaStat without stopping the cycling seizures, we took him by ambulance to the local hospital. The ER doctor there contacted Dr. Barnes to see what was next on the "to do" list. He noted that Caleb's continual pattern of uncontrolled seizures, a normal day for Caleb, was what they would consider a "Status" episode. He offered to keep us over night, but Caleb was exhausted after the seizures finally slowed, and sleep was a rare commodity, so I asked to take him home but promised to come back if anything progressed.

We saw Dr. Barnes again on the 19th and his VNS was adjusted again and we adjusted medications again to try to slow down the seizures and to increase his alertness during the day and to help him rest at night. It was a tall order, but Dr. Barnes was hopeful the new VNS adjustment might help. He also said "Sleep, sleep is good." We quote him on that to this day! And he is so right, during the stress of the everyday regimen and the restlessness and seizures that Caleb endured daily, sleep was a precious thing. So we were hopeful that rest was something that could be gained, and a reduction in seizures would be seen.

Tuesdays were blood draw days and Ms. Patsy and Ms. Sherrie were always there at the outpatient lab and were so good to Caleb. They would always get the needle in on the first try and they were always cheerful and sweet to Caleb. He had become a "celebrity" of sorts there, sad you are so well known at the hospital, but nevertheless, they always made the best of a tough situation. And of course, sweet Caleb, he was a trooper and always did great.

A sore throat and an upper respiratory infection came along, and wheezing continued as well. Caleb was back on antibiotics again. His little body was so tired even before the illness, and now he was just absolutely lethargic. It was sad, but we were doing everything humanly possible to keep him going, all of us were working to try to keep him as well as we could, but the hopelessness was starting to set in.

The family dynamics at home were difficult too. The girls would spend their days at school, Chad at work, and then when they came home to the place that was supposed to be predictable and relaxing, it was instead a: high stress, unpredictable, Caleb's health regimen controlled zone. For me it was normal, but the stress was overwhelming sometimes. Many times we were all just emotional wrecks! Nana and Papa usually stepped in to take the girls to their house on the weekends. My sister and brothers and their families would also step in and pick up the slack wherever it was needed. Aunt Ellen and Uncle Jason would come to take them shopping or to a party, to church or they and John and Jessica would be "stand in parents" when we were at the hospital. David and Elizabeth would plan weekends where the girls could stay with them to try to give them some individual attention. The whole family did their best to try to help. Ellen and Nana had spent countless days helping me at home, and at the hospital. We were so blessed to have a supportive and giving family to help us through.

It was just an awful feeling to not be able to be with the girls when they needed us. Chad also felt helpless because he was constantly having to work. But no money, no doctors visits, no insurance, you know the cycle. So I told him to think of how much him having a good job was truly helping us all and he tried, but I know it was hard for him too.

Sleepless nights continued, and we had to enlist friends to get the girls to school for us in the mornings…another thing I couldn't do for them. However, I realized how blessed we were to have such great friends in our lives who would help us with the girls so I could care for Caleb.

Many mornings he would wake up during the wee hours and then go to sleep right when it was time to get the girls up. Some days even when Caleb tried to sleep, the seizures would be so intense they would wake him. It was tiring for him to seize, but if he slept, he would seize. It was a vicious cycle.

Chapter 9: Feeding, Frailty and Faith

Caleb's myoclonic seizures were anywhere from 200 to 500 in a day by mid fall. His lethargic state was back and he overall was just deteriorating cognitively, no speech, and very little activity. I would set and think through his day and chart everything: sleep or no sleep, clusters of seizures, tired or more awake, constipated or diarrhea, cognitively with us or not. I came to the conclusion that there was no rhyme or reason, there was no sure way of knowing where we would be the next day, or the next moment for that matter. But still there I would go trying to figure out any pattern, any correlation, anything tangible to be able to reason - why?

By mid- September Caleb was surviving most days on yogurt and baby food. It would take me all day to feed him. He would sit in his wheelchair and seize continually while I tried to feed him. It was terrible. Some days I could get little bites of food in better than others, so I felt like that it was something that neurologically coincided with "bad seizure days".

He also went into Status again and we had to use DiaStat, this time it slowed the seizures, and we were grateful. The realization that going to the hospital really didn't help had sunk in. That fact was overwhelming. Most of the time when your child is ill there is some comfort knowing that there are doctors that can "make it all better". Knowing that our child would never be "all better" was tough, especially when you left the hospital with no improvement, but just a "calming of the storm." We knew everyone was trying their very best to help him.

Illnesses seemed to keep creeping in, and for every action we took to get rid of the infection, seizures would increase. And then if he was coherent and not lethargic, and seemed to be "feeling" better, then he would be shoving his hands in his mouth, beating on the door to go for a ride, or trying to climb up the window! And then the next moment he might not be able to even stand. Most of the time the nervous activity would precipitate seizures. It was hard to watch, and sometimes we would just pray for the seizure to break through so he could relax.

Vomiting up food started becoming par for the course with Caleb as well. I would smash his food and even puree things to try to get him to eat on tough seizure days. Some days I would work for hours to get a small amount of food in, and then it would just come right back up.

October 18th, 2008- We started Caleb on a medication from Canada. We were so hopeful for this to work as his seizure activity was increasing by the day.

October also brought more respiratory problems, so we started albuterol treatments and we continued increasing the Canadian meds for the increase in seizures. He also began vomiting up his meds continually, so we started medication for acid reflux in hopes that this would help.

November 7th, 2008, was Caleb's 7th birthday. We celebrated with all the family on the 8th since there are lots of November birthdays.

I got weepy every time we sang "Happy Birthday" to Caleb, it was the milestone of yet another year that we were blessed enough to have him here with us. This particular birthday, Caleb slept through most of it. He was weak and couldn't hold his head up well. He was blessed with many presents and cards from across the country. Many had heard of us through his Caringbridge site and were people we'd never met, but who had become part of Team Caleb!

We had several doctors appointments in November, and it seemed that the Canadian medication was starting to help some with at least Caleb's tonics seizure numbers coming down some, so it was a welcome improvement. We were praying immediately that it would last! While the tonic numbers were decreasing however, his myoclonic seizures were the worst numbers ever, up to 750 one day, and I was having to massage his throat to help him swallow his food. At this point I had researched feeding problems with children with severe neurological impairments, and I read about G-tubes, I was concerned this was where we were headed, but it was not what I wanted for our sweet boy.

Caringbridge Update, Monday, November 24th, 2008

Team Caleb,
Thanks for all your prayers for Caleb. I am really concerned about his health at this point. We increased tranxene back up to 3xday as ordered by Dr. Barnes, Sat. I am trying to be patient with the meds. However, he is walking like his legs are made with Jell-O, and I don't think he could swallow Jell-O if

he wanted to. I am entertaining allowing him dairy again just to get some liquid calories back in him. His diet consists of finely chopped bacon, his favorite, and I can only get down about 1/8 of a cup, that's not much folks, at one time. He loves food, he loves to eat, he just can't. There is something about your child not eating that hurts on a very personal level. You know when you bring your newborn home that they must eat to thrive. Caleb and I failed at nursing, and I am feeling those same feelings now as I reach for a jar of baby food. Sat. night it hit me so hard, I had an absolute meltdown over a jar of vegetable turkey dinner. I was so glad he could swallow it and he ate 1/2 a jar. And then the reality that my 7 year old can only get down baby food sunk in. I wept for probably 1/2 an hour, the whole time it took him to get it down. I wish there was an answer or a simple fix, but this has slowly been going downhill, it has just worsened over the last two weeks to monumental status. I am hoping the increase in meds helps, but right now, I am not very optimistic. He is attempting to play again. He played for 30 min. this morning but after eating 3 pieces of diced peaches, he was out like a light. He is sleeping so much. He sleeps at least 10 to 11 hours a night and then has 1 1/2 hr. morning nap and around the same in the afternoon. Which leaves about 10 hours to have over 500 myoclonic seizures and to attempt to feed him and guide him through the house so he doesn't bounce off the furniture. I pray this is a phase. But my gut says different, and I don't want to listen to it. How many times do you have to lose parts of your child? We lost so much with autism, then seizures, then speech, then mobility, then comprehension, then more mobility issues, then to fatigue, now he won't eat. And the seizures persist, and right now I am angry that he has to deal with this, my Caleb is fighter, but it seems his spunk is fading and I am trying to be strong but the reality of it is smacking me in the face. Right now he is attempting to play trucks while laying on the floor. I know feeding is coming again then meds and another nap, so I need to get it going. Please pray this inability is temporary and is lifted from his load. He loves to eat, and it pains me when I know he's hungry and can't get it down. We are trying all the tricks in the book, but he is almost too tired to even try. I don't like where this could go, so please pray at least this could go away.

Meanwhile, I will be patient and be thankful that Team Caleb is there for us, and that my two healthy girls are thriving, and that we are very blessed regardless of the circumstances. Caleb is a blessing and the Lord has given us more than we have need. I love you all. Beth.

December 1st, 2008, After Caleb would not eat for a few days and then would not drink one day, I called Dr. Barnes and he recommended that we get to Vandy to get Team Caleb there to help us out! His oxygen levels were low when we got there and continued to be, they put him on oxygen to help and did x-rays to determine that he had acquired Aspiration Pneumonia. They worked on him with respiratory therapy. This was a new field for me to learn about, so I started researching as soon as I could get my hands on a computer. They were doing chest percussion to loosen up the congestion. They began doing extra breathing treatments as well. We met with Neurology and they discussed the fact that the pneumonia could be the reason for all the increase in the myoclonic activity. We also discussed with them the need for him to receive his medications. He had been vomiting them up for some time off and on now, and was also vomiting up food. He also was having severe deficits in swallowing since August, so there were so many things going wrong at once, it was difficult to know where to start. However, receiving medication and nourishment were paramount. So a NG tube was placed. This went through his nose into his stomach. This allowed us to get his medication in.

He was given a swallow study and we watched as liquids and foods were aspirated right into his lungs on x-ray. We were concerned he wouldn't even try to eat, but he accepted the fact that he needed to, and he slowly opened his mouth and allowed us to put barium laden foods into him. It was sad for me to see him aspirate this and as we did the test I remember thinking "great, more stuff we need to get out of his lungs now." Bless his heart, we plugged him back into the NG tube.

A G-tube would be the answer to enable us to get medication and nourishment to him. It was not the step we wanted for him. But his body was trying to tell us that he was no longer able to feed like he used to. It was hard to take, but it was necessary. I knew immediately that I would miss fixing him bacon and letting him eat mountains of Puffcorn. And I was concerned that he would miss it too. We didn't eat in front of Caleb at this point. I could not let him see us eat and be changing the way that he would be eating. I was trying to focus on what he would be able to do, and with a G-tube, he would be able to get stronger and not sleep incessantly, and hopefully seizures would slow and we would be able to insure that he didn't aspirate food or medication. We discussed all this with the attending pediatrician. She told us to get ready for a long stay and settle in.

Caleb continued to have problems with his oxygen level being low. He had another x-ray and then an upper GI to test for reflux. He didn't reflux on the upper GI study, however, once back in the room he had started vomiting and his NG tube worked its way up his esophagus. Also, when respiratory came by to suction out his lungs she pulled milk from his NG feeds out of his lungs. He clearly was refluxing the milk back up through his esophagus and into his lungs. The nurses and doctors spoke and decided to make it NJ, this would be from his nose down to his small intestine. Hopefully this would keep him from "refluxing" out the tube. It was so awful to see him uncomfortable, and the tube and all the worries and problems with it, just made us that more hopeful that the G-tube would truly help.

The surgery team came up and spoke with me and I pushed to have the reflux issue fixed by them going ahead and doing a fundoplication. This is a procedure where the stomach is "tied off" at the top where it joins the esophagus. I felt strongly that it was necessary, especially with the continual bouts of vomiting. I had read about the procedure and we were nervous about it, but it seemed like an inevitable progression of Caleb's continual regression. It was so hard to accept that we were at this point. Yet, we were grateful that there was some thing that could be done to help this.

From dealing with irretractible epilepsy, where there is little hope for control, at least with the circumstances there was something that could "fix" this problem. The surgery happened on Wednesday, December 10th, and it went well. When the surgeon came out, he said there was severe signs of reflux and we were right in doing the fundoplication along with the G-tube placement. He said Caleb had come through the procedure well and explained what we would see.

The waiting room and the hospital were full of "TEAM CALEB" members donning their t-shirts. Many of our favorite Vandy staff team members, Dr. Barnes, Mary Montgomery, Alisha Morgan, Ginny Collier and others checked in on him. We were surrounded with cards, balloons and prayers from people across the country. It was amazing and so humbling to feel such love.

Caleb did not sleep well the night after surgery and we thought it was from pain. We had pushed his button for his pain medication, but didn't realize we could have pushed it more frequently. He was pinching and grasping with his arms and I was afraid we hadn't stayed ahead of the pain and so we stayed up through the wee hours of the morning pushing his pain button for him in hopes he would relax.

By early morning the respiratory therapist had come by and said he sounded awful. In three hours she had come in 4 times to work on him. He was struggling. His oxygen started to drop and they had to bag him and get him to the ICU to get him the care he needed. I hadn't been apart from Caleb, I wouldn't even leave the room- thanks to Aunt Ellen, and Nana, they would always go do the running and I wouldn't have to leave him. But, this was him struggling and they told me to give them 30 minutes to get him settled and to let them work on him and then I could come in. It was the longest 30 minutes of my life. Here is Aunt Ellen's Caringbridge entry from the ordeal: it happened on Dec. 12th, but Ellen couldn't bring herself to journal it until the 14th:

Caringbridge entry, Sunday December 14th, 2008:

Team Caleb---

Last night when I talked with Beth they had all been moved and settled into room 7413. The attending Dr. had then come up from PCCU to answer her questions. She apologized for not getting to her before they left but they had MANY critical patients, which is completely understandable. Beth asked her what the consensus was on Caleb's respiratory distress, how and why he had problems that caused the 'event' on Thursday. She explained it was for several reasons, his pre-existing pneumonia didn't help, also the intubation during surgery can impact respiratory for some children and can cause his lungs to collapse, and the morphine on top of all of this can again cause respiratory issues. This plus the fact that he had rebuilt some fluid in the lower lobes of his lungs= respiratory distress for him. The current plan is a forced air albuterol treatment(which Caleb has been responding well to) every 6 hours or

more if needed, percussion therapy, and suctioning if needed. Beth said he was coughing up stuff after his first one! This is great news because Caleb can't really cough by choice or command, he needed something to force it up, and these type treatments have seemed to help. The sections of his upper right lung that were debated if collapsed or just much as deposits are fine and look good, whichever they were. He is breathing on only a 1/2 liter of oxygen and staying at 95-98 %, which is better than he has been in weeks! Beth said he breaths better now after all this than before, so that is great news!

Dr. Barnes came in yesterday as well. He had been following all of Caleb's daily struggles as well. He was exactly who Beth had been wanting to see! He suggest that nothing is done right now, but before Caleb goes home, he wants to wean the depokene, and also lower the VNS, yes, Lower....this is the first time he has ever felt it should be turned down. I guess to help eliminate any possibility of it affecting his recovery. Also he spoke to Beth about Caleb's Ketogenic Diet. This will of course go in the G-tube, and hopefully Caleb will be able to produce Ketones, which can help the number of seizures he has each day decrease. We know he is very sensitive with this diet before, but now it should be easier to at least try it since the G-tube is in. Dr. Barnes said that he would let everyone else do their thing to get him as well as they could, and then he would address the neurological side of things before Caleb comes home.

HERE IS THE RUNDOWN OF THURSDAY A.M.(Grab the tissues)

So, Wed. night Mama and I had traded back off, and Caleb went to sleep around 11 or so. Beth and I quickly followed him to sleep as well. This was the day of Caleb's G-tube and nissan surgeries Caleb had a morphine pump that was controlled by a button for pain. Since Caleb can't tell us he wants us to push the button, Beth and I said we would push it if he woke up, or made any sounds of discomfort. Around 3 in the morning, Caleb was laughing and it woke me up. The sweetest little giggly voice, but I wasn't laughing cause I knew it was a gelastic seizure. It lasted over a minute followed by 2 short ones. Beth stayed asleep so, I was thrilled for that. After he seized he just laid there and seemed uncomfortable, so, I pushed his pain meds. I wondered, how often we could do this, and hoped he hadn't been in pain from 11till 3. I also thought, we should probably push it again in an hour. So, I stayed up till 4. At 4 I pushed it and the nurses came in to do vitals. Caleb was still not asleep, he had just been laying motionless. The nurse informed me we could have been pushing him morphine every 10 minutes. WOW, I thought, he hasn't been getting hardly anything then. so I stayed up till 5 and had pushed it 3 times in that hour, thinking "this will help him out, poor thing" Beth woke up around 5 and continued the same after I told her what the nurse had said. Caleb by this point was restless and agitated, we accredited it to pain, and blamed ourselves for not staying ahead of the pain, and now trying to play catch -up.

Around 6:30 the regular routine of Dr.'s flowing in began.

Caleb was still on the nasal cannula of oxygen, but was seeming more and more upset and panicked. He had begun to squeeze Beth's hands. Shift change was at 7 and when our nurse came in at 8:30 again to check on us, we told her he wasn't acting right, something was WRONG. She watched for a few minutes and his saturation levels were dropping then, she bumped up his oxygen and waited. He did okay, so she left was in and out of our room for the next hour, too many times to count. She put a mask on him, bumped up his oxygen again and called respiratory.

At 9 respiratory had come by. This nurse was determined that Caleb wasn't going "downstairs" and that was the first time ICU was in the air as a possibility. We didn't really entertain the notion, because he had finally calmed. It was not out of the question for his sats to drop when he was sleeping, they had off and on several nights. It wasn't surprising that he needed a O2 mask. He usually had at night. What did surprise us was that 10 minutes after the respiratory was done and left, Caleb's breathing sounded awful! She had suctioned him thru both nasal openings and down the throat, she listened to him and that sounded good, and here less then 10 minutes later was a dark raspy breathing we hadn't heard before, ever. So his nurse was back, suctioned him herself and got even more dark, thick, mucus.

We saw this continue from 9:30 till almost 11. I cannot remember how many times they would think he was good and then a couple breaths later, wheezy or raspy noises would start right back up. It was as if when they suctioned him, his lungs automatically made more. Somewhere in the middle of all of this chaos, a chest x-ray was ordered. It seemed, they were done; the Dr. for the floor had been in and said that she felt like he was okay now, but if he was needing to be suctioned so frequently he would need to be down on ICU or PCCU as they call it. She explained that they are just better equipped to do an hourly suctioning. He would need to go from now till 1 without any problems to avoid this.

We, took some deep breaths and we were relieved that Caleb was asleep and holding his sats for the moment. He rested for an hour and we called Chad and Nana to tell them the days drama, and give the, a 'heads up' if Caleb got worse. And he did. He woke at almost one hour exactly and was breathing horribly. The nurse came in and paged the Dr. for the floor, respiratory was there, and then the Dr. from the surgery team showed up (he was coming by the assessment of what he had heard from the morning). He was concerned, and Caleb was on 90% oxygen in a matter of minutes. Caleb was still dropping in the O2 department. I remember the nurse briefly going over everything quickly with him, he asked for a chest x-ray and she told him we had one done earlier that showed okay.

Beth was sitting on the edge of the bed, and I think I was pacing the floor at this point. Now, I had complete tunnel vision, I knew there were 4-5 people in the room, but I could see only Caleb, he was getting worse...quickly, each breath seemed to be a harder struggle, I could feel myself trying to take deep breaths for him, only to notice my pulse was racing and adrenaline had set in. Each time his breath was shallower, and then he started making awful noises, when he would breathe, it wasn't a wheeze anymore, more of a gasping sound, and I heard someone say "look at his chest."

I focused totally on his chest only to see the cavity of his chest almost fully collapsing with each attempt to get a breath in, someone else said "bump up his oxygen" to which the nurse replied " it is at 100%." I heard the Dr. from Surgery say, "he needs to be transported to PCCU....call the transport team now, and get the crash cart in here." Tunnel vision was gone, I now saw a room full of people, 10 or more, I bumped someone as I moved backwards away from Caleb, as it seemed I was getting bumped and shoved where I was standing.

I moved over to a small area where no one was, Caleb was still struggling and I took a look around the room, long faces, panicked faces, and concern on faces. Faces of Dr.'s and nurses who had seen this 1,000 times I am sure, but I had never seen them so panicked.

They were obviously doing all they could, but Caleb couldn't do anymore.

The transport team was there very quick, we gave Caleb a kiss each, and the floor Dr. we had seen before came in and explained things quickly to Beth, then transport told her she could come down and join them in 30 minutes. They also bagged him at this point and said if that didn't work they may have to call anesthesia to do an intubation and needed her consent to do so. They wheeled Caleb out, and the respiratory nurse we had helping Caleb all morning asked Beth if she was going to be okay...which Beth replied to tearfully for the first time "yeah, i will be fine".

We sat down together, as the room emptied from 10 nurses and doctors to just us. We had lost our breath too it seemed. I asked Beth what she needed and she said "an O2 mask "...we had a chuckle followed by a good cry.

A couple of nurses came in to check on us, and the apologies began, each nurse apologizing as if they had done something wrong. We hurried to pack up a week and a half of clothes, cards, food, the whole collection. We had a pile of going to ICU and going to the car. I made fast trips to the car and threw things in. On my last trip, the 30 minutes had expired and Beth was going downstairs to be with Caleb. Our nurse , and our respiratory nurse, who was determined not to have Caleb downstairs, sat there as we left, apologizing. Beth said "its okay, he will be fine now and thank you" They looked like they took this personally, and i felt bad for that. We knew they tried so hard.

They let Beth in at 3 to see Caleb, and it was about 4 before I got back there. I was relieved to see him on the Bipap and not intubated. He was at 100% forced air at that time. I made sure Beth had taken extra steroids, so she didn't crash. And she had. We stayed at his bedside, relived to see him resting and not struggling. The rest you know...... In addition, we are thankful he is out of PCCU so fast! There have been many days with Caleb, I never want to re-live. This particular one ranks tops.

Thank You all for your prayers, it is what got all of us thru this past Thursday and sustains us each day we know. Your cards, ecards, food, gifts, and ect. are all appreciated.
"Cast thy burden upon the Lord, and he shall sustain thee: he shall never suffer the righteous to be moved" Ps 55:22
"He giveth power to the faint; and to them that have no might, he increaseth strength" Isaiah 40 :29
Love to all--Aunt Ellen

Meanwhile, throughout all of this, Caleb's seizures were relentless. One night in the ICU he clustered seizures continually, we counted over 1000 myoclonic seizures and the tonic seizures were breaking through as well. Finally, some IV Valium gave him a bit of relief. The next morning Dr. Barnes came by and said, "When everyone else gets done with him, we are going to try some things to help." So I was glad there was a plan! We also had decided with Mary Montgomery to restart Caleb on the Ketogenic diet now that he would be G-tube fed. It was a no-brainer. It was so important for him to get nourishment and seizure control. This could potentially give him both, and since being tube fed would be more consistent and specific, we were hoping that Caleb would respond favorably.

Finally, his lungs had turned around and he was on room air, it was a true blessing! We started the diet and were starting to see the last rounds of all the specialists. We knew going home was on the agenda, so we were so grateful. We had made some changes to his seizure medications and the VNS settings again, and were going home with him on bolus (a set volume going in slowly with gravity) feeds of the ketogenic diet through his G-tube. His lungs were sounding better and we were doing breathing treatments as well to continue to keep him clear.

We made it home by the 16th. We were thankful to be home, but I wished I could just take Mary and Dr. Barnes home with us sometimes! However, we made it and getting used to all the "new routine" took a couple of days, but we made it!

After we were home for a few days, Caleb's seizure counts dropped to around 100 daily, I never thought I would welcome 100 seizures in a day, but when I'd seen him have 1000, this was a welcome thought. We were seeing him be more awake throughout the day and have energy enough to watch Barney and at least sit up on the couch and turn the wheels on his trucks. I know that doesn't sound like much, but when you've seen your child completely lethargic, Barney and some wheels were a HUGE improvement!

Psalms 28:7 "The Lord is my strength and my shield; my heart trusted in Him, and I am helped: therefore my heart greatly rejoiceth; and with my song I will praise Him." - We knew that Caleb was still sick, still weak and frail, but we had him still with us, and that alone was worth all the thanks we could give the Lord for helping us through.

Seizure Log Caleb Baker 2008

Month	myoclonic	tonic	totals
Jan.		73	83
Feb.	739 some tonic		739
Mar.	1441	45	1487
Apr.	6549	144	6693
May.	8318	324	8642
Jun.	5151	243	5394
Jul.	5401	487	5888
Aug.	7100	178	7278
Sept.	7470	196	7666
Oct.	9940	807	10747
Nov.	11000	302	11347
Dec.	5718	202	6273

Chapter 10: Rolling With The Punches: G-tubes, GI and Ice Storms

Christmas approached quickly and we were overwhelmed with kindness, gifts, cards and most of all expressions of love from near and far. It was a wonderful time to be with all of the family. It was hard on Caleb, and we just made sure that even if we were at a different place, that he had a room to himself where he could lay and watch his shows and have quiet. A friend of ours, Audrey, came to help with him at Christmas too, so that we could spend time with the family and Caleb could still be happy. He was still unable to stand or do his wobbly walk, but we were hopeful that it was just from the weakness and that he would get some of that back.

He was tolerating his feeds well, and while he still had the large port for now, we were learning to deal with the new way of "feeding" Caleb. From the moment we began tube feeds, I gave him a large tube to hold while I gave him his feeds. This seemed to preoccupy his hands so they didn't decide to grasp the tube with the feeds in them so I was glad that it worked.

By the 30th of December though, Caleb's lungs were diminished again and an x-ray showed early stages of pneumonia. On January 1st, he was no better and after speaking with Dr. Mudd in Paducah, he advised us to get him back to Vandy. The ER got us in quickly and did an x-ray and let me see it. It looked similar to one taken the day after his surgery, so it was not good. Since he had a fundoplication and g-tube it was unlikely that he was aspirating on feeds, but it was possible that he was aspirating on his own secretions.

An upper GI was done to ensure that the fundoplication was in place and functioning properly, and it was. So then the obvious, sinus infection, was the culprit of this pneumonia. We discussed with the attending pediatrician, that keeping Caleb "germ free" was necessary. We decided to also restart OT and PT at home to try to keep him "moving" some to keep him as strong as possible so that "settling" in his lungs was less likely. He finally improved and we were dismissed to the surgery clinic where they put in Caleb's Mic-Key button (a smaller and easier port for his g-tube). We were glad to have that done and headed home....

But this time coming home meant a change for everyone. In an effort to keep germs away from Caleb there was a strict hand washing regimen placed on all who entered our home. Also, we asked for anyone who had been around kids, school, any public place, to either change clothes or wear a hospital gown over their clothes if they were going to be near Caleb. We also asked anyone who was sick or who had been sick not to visit. This was a big change. However, after reading about Chronic Pulmonary Aspiration and realizing this is what Caleb was dealing with on top of his Epilepsy, it was necessary.

We weekly touched base with Dr. Barnes and Mary to adjust medications or feeds as necessary for optimum results. It was a daunting task to take notes daily of everything that he did, how his seizures were and how his feeds/GI issues were, and now we added respiratory notes to the chart.

Medications and machines were piling into our home at warp speed. A suction machine accompanied the nebulizer in the room. I was glad to not have to use it immediately to suction him, but found that it was great for brushing his teeth and suctioning out everything- at least that wouldn't go to his lungs too.

Caleb was beginning to whine frequently, and we suspected it was him being more coherent and him sensing seizure activity since shortly after the seizures would begin. His numbers were still holding around 100 daily, through January, so we were encouraged that this could possibly continue. We were hopeful that the ketogenic diet was helping.

We met with Dr. Barnes for our check-up and he rejoiced with us in the seizure improvement and told us to keep him updated. He also discussed with us the chronic aspiration and we discussed tracheotomy. I knew that medically this was the only way to prevent aspiration indefinitely, however, a tracheotomy would present other problems that come with it. So, Chad and I hoped we wouldn't have to deal with this, and that somehow he would improve.

But January brought a runny nose, and then another pneumonia, so we combated it with antibiotics and hoped it would quickly turn things around so we could miss out on the hospital for at least a month!

Meanwhile, between breathing treatments and chest percussion 4 times a day, meds and feeds, I was trying to find time to do things with my girls, but time was something that was a rare commodity! Many of the family would "fill in" for me and help so I could get away just to take them to shop or to the library for some peaceful time.

Caleb's whining and agitation was continual some days. And the fact that there was nothing I could do to help him was overwhelming as a mom. On days like that sometimes I would just sit with him and cry with him. On other days, he might be a bit more mobile and "limp" around the house whining. His legs and feet had started turning in and becoming extremely difficult for him to balance on. But we wanted to encourage movement as much as possible so we'd just wobble with him. Some days he was so agitated that he'd claw, pinch and pull at us constantly. Increasing his Tranxene seemed to help a bit sometimes... but not every time.

January 26th, 2009, an ICE STORM hit Paducah. We were doing breathing treatments and suctioning secretions in the car with an AC adapter. Meanwhile, in and out of the house we were dodging limbs that were falling in the yard because of the weight of the ice. We received Caleb's feeds via UPS- they truly deliver in rain, snow and ICE. After a second round of more ice, we left the next morning for a hotel. Doing Caleb's routine feeds, meds and breathing treatment schedule were easier there, but the stress of trying to secure gas and food in Paducah was becoming evident and we decided to head south to Nashville.

We are so blessed to have family, James and Amy Boggess and their sweet kids who live there and opened their home to us! It was fun for our girls to be with their cousins. I kept Caleb and his routine going and Nana,Ellen and Zeb went with us to help. Chad worked in Union City, TN which is an hour drive from Paducah, so rather than deal with the ice he got a hotel room close to work and stayed there until the weekend and drove home to start working on clearing the roof and yard of debris. We finally had power restored on February 7th, so we were so thankful to be back home and were grateful that we could take care of Caleb's needs in his "familiar" place - HOME!

During the storm we staved off secretions by the respiratory routine, and his seizures seemed to stay around the 100 mark, so stability was a good thing during such a stressful time. Caleb was walking a bit more some days and that was good to see. He was very attached to me- but I loved it. After all the hospitalizations I guess he was insecure about where he was and what was happening, but Mommy was there, and I was so thankful that me being there was a comfort to him in some way.

Retching, (the act of vomiting- but nothing could come up because of the fundoplication) started happening regularly for Caleb, and some days he was just weak from it. He'd break a sweat and then just be exhausted. Eventually he'd have a terribly sick diarrhea diaper and "rid" himself of whatever had upset his tummy. He also had lost a bit of weight so Mary increased his formula again to try to help him get some more calories in.

He seemed to be more stable in February as far as seizures go, and we were continually grateful. One battle we were trying to deal with was his sensory issues and we used lots of singing and compression techniques as guided by our excellent OT. They were excellent with Caleb and we were so glad to have them in our home to work with Caleb. Our lead OT had worked with Caleb since he was little and when he was still verbal. She was so good to him and worked with us and with him at wherever he was at. That is tough for lots of therapists to understand about neurologically challenged children. But they "got it" and we were so blessed to have them to help. Our PT therapists, were also good with him and when all he could do was just lay in the floor then they would just do all they could with him right there!

Caleb became obsessed with "RED". Red toys, red objects, red shirts…if you were wearing a red shirt- you were fair game! You might be pinched or slobbery when he got through with you too! Bless his heart, red was the first color he learned.

He continued to have lots of "stuff" in his lungs but we kept it loose and we were grateful that we had the tools to do so. I finally taught Chad how to feed Caleb, being the control freak that I am, that was tough to do, but it was time for him to step in and help and learn. He did pretty well, and it was a blessing to have extra hands.

Caleb had been walking a bit more off and on during his day and one day he walked into the kitchen. At this point we were still not eating in front of him at all. I was terrified. I didn't want him to go to the microwave (asking for bacon) or go to the refrigerator (for a juice box). He didn't. He walked to the towel where I had his tubes and syringes drying after they'd been cleaned. He picked up the tube that I let him hold while I did his feedings, and he brought it to me- as to say, "I'm hungry." It was the most precious thing, and he was right, it was time for a feeding. Right then I realized that this precious boy, regardless of what neurological issues he was dealing with, was able to adjust to whatever was next in the regressive steps his body was taking. I stood in awe of him, and still do to this day. There was nothing that he was unable to adapt to.

March presented Caleb with more battles. He developed strep, as Camille had picked it up from school and been ill. So we were even more so adamant about hand washing and germs. The biggest battle was the constant of Caleb putting his hands in his mouth…and there was nothing to stop him from it. So we just worked diligently at cleaning his hands frequently. His strep developed into pneumonia, again. And the realization of where he was, respiratory wise, was sinking in. Our pediatrician and Dr. Barnes recommended that we begin seeing a pulmonologist at Vandy. So we started being followed by Dr. Paul Moore. He was very kind to Caleb and very helpful. He was also extremely compassionate and down to earth. We knew we were being blessed by having another of "the best" on Team Caleb!

Tests were done to check his lungs, meanwhile we started another antibiotic of Clyndamycin to try to clear him up. This was becoming routine since December and I was greatly concerned at how the effects of all the repetitive antibiotic treatments would carry out. But it was necessary to help him clear all the infection, as he was at this point, unable to "get over" anything on his own.

Caleb's continual whining and moaning was almost more than I could bear some days. It was just agony for him I know, and yet there was little I could do to help him. He was very tired, but on occasion, after playing "creepy mouse" with him or watching and singing Barney to him, or when someone he recognized came in, you might get a quick glimpse of a grin- and that was priceless. The smallest of things had become very big accomplishments for Caleb and for us.

Caleb would have frequent GI issues as well. Retching became an issue at night time, so we reduced his feeds before bed to try to help. He was losing weight as well, so Mary, our dietician was constantly adjusting his feed formula to get the most calories and fats as possible. She was always thinking about him and trying to help keep his ketones elevated while working to "fatten him up" too!

There were some issues as well with constipation for him. There was never a balance for Caleb as far as his bowels, we always seemed to dance between constipation and diarrhea. If Caleb's seizures increased he would become more constipated, sometimes unable to go for days, which at times would require me to give him enemas. Those are just no fun. When Caleb was on antibiotics for a while, (which was seeming to happen monthly with all the respiratory issues) he would inevitably have rounds of constant diarrhea. There was no happy medium any more.

Chapter 11: Calm Waters and Agonizing Reality

We were on another round of antibiotics by the end of March and we were trying to keep Caleb well enough to go on a family vacation to North Carolina. We were going with most of my family and a group of close friends. We'd had it planned for a year, and we tried to make it comfortable and fun for Caleb. Thankfully, he was some better and with doing his respiratory treatments four times daily- everyday, we were able to go. It was a blessing. Caleb loved water. He used to lay on his back in the bathtub when he was little so that only his eyes, nose and mouth peeked out of the bubbles, he was the cutest thing! He really enjoyed swimming too. At one time we had his OT to do water therapy with him to calm him and give him great sensory input. He was not able to swim, but he liked for us to "swim" him around and his favorite was the hot tub!

At the beach, we were able to borrow a beach wheelchair for Caleb from the local fire department. It was wonderful. He was able to watch the waves come in and stroll along with us everywhere on the sand. The only problem was the wet wheels were covered in sand and he loved wheels too, so he would reach down to touch the wheel and then his hands would go right back in his mouth! But he enjoyed it so much, especially the hot tub. We took turns getting in with him. He relaxed so much one day that he went to sleep while we were holding him in the hot tub, which resulted in him seizing, but for him to relax at all was such a blessing to see. Most of Caleb's day he spent with every muscle in his body tensed, his hands in his mouth, or grinding his teeth and just being anxious with discomfort. It was so hard to see. So to see his hands come out of his mouth long enough to touch the water, gave us great joy and comfort that he was being comforted even a little.

We enjoyed relaxing on our trip. Chad and I discovered though, how overwhelming Caleb's care had become. He was mobile enough that he would crawl around to get things, and sometimes try to do his wobbly walk. So we had to literally be with him at all times. This meant a great deal of isolation from the group. Caleb didn't like noise, loud talking, and he needed room to "roll around" and play with his wheels. So it was me, Chad and Papa continually taking turns to be with him. When I wasn't with him I was mixing feeds or readying medications or getting breathing treatments set up. I was realizing that there was little rest, even on vacation, because regardless of where we were, Caleb's schedule remained the same. We were grateful to have a nice home to visit with our family and to be able to share time with our children at the ocean. It is amazing how the ocean soothes the soul.

Caringbridge entry, Monday April 13, 2009:

Team Caleb---
* Tissue Warning*(for you uncle Day Day)
We are home after a long visit at Caleb's Dr.'s.
His appointment was at 1:40, we were called back at 2..saw the first Fellow, at 3 and then saw Dr. Moore at 3:20. So needless to say. They were busy and running behind. Caleb did great though. And while we were waiting he took a nap.
The Fellow looked Caleb over good, said his ears were a little pink, but otherwise he seemed okay. She could hear some movements in his lungs. So, that was good too, although we wanted her to be able to hear what Beth hears at home. But, that's the way it goes. She talked with Beth for a while about how Caleb's health was overall, and then asked Beth " what is your Medical background?" To which Beth answered "just a Google MD and a lot of hands on research in the Autism and then Neuro/seizure fields. I am new to Respiratory" ...the Dr. just laughed and said "well your doing great then."
A few minutes later Dr.Moore came in...he is a GREAT Dr. He talked with Beth and I about Caleb and how he has been continually developing this aspiration stuff. He said to continue the chest percussions and he bumped up those to 3 times a day...4 if he is having a hard day. Then he added the albuterol instead of the pulmicort. He thought this was helping more. Beth agreed. She told him Caleb's seizures have been heading back up in #'s lately and he has been running a low temp off and on...so she thought he was starting to get pneumonia again. He listened to his lungs and said he wanted a chest X-ray. They

weren't bad per say, but not too clear either and he wanted to see what the film showed. He also added a blood gas check to his already ordered weekly blood draw for today.

Then, he started to talk about where all of this is heading...he said that in the next few months if Caleb is worse and has to be hospitalized again that he will run a Bronchiectomy (sp?) test. This will be done under anesthesia, just to make sure that nothing else is going on besides the aspiration. He said that if nothing else shows up, then we will know we are dealing with just the aspiration....there are some "radical" choices such as a Tracheotomy or Botox injections in his throat. Beth told him she was fine with anything that would HELP Caleb...that she had come to terms the fact he might have to have one. Dr. Moore then said " I want you to talk to some other parents first who have been in your place...in the age of technology, sometimes we (as Dr.'s) are quick to throw out these "radical" ideas that DO help...but short term..and parents want to do that...and later regret doing so, because they have a quality of life issue..they have just prolonged their child's suffering..........I want you to know that I am not opposed to a natural progression of things...we both acknowledge this (respiratory issue) has been caused from other problems he has...most of my patients have other illness and the lungs are the last natural order/organ to be affected." Beth and I were both crying and she said " I needed someone in a white coat to say that...I am just wrestling with what is best for Caleb right now...his days are mostly spent unhappy, and I am trying so hard just to be able to keep him at home" Dr. Moore and the

Fellow shook their heads in agreement and Dr. Moore said again.." it eventually becomes a quality of life discussion...we aren't there just yet...when we get to that point...I will sit down with Dr. Barnes and we will discuss and then you and all your support people will have a conference...we will talk to you about anything left we can do, and you will have some tough decisions to make." Beth still talking with a shaking voice some how had the strength to mutter out "That is what I need to know, how bad are his lungs, from one year ago...his overall health is just so much worse....". Dr. Moore said "oh..Caleb will let us know when it is time, I can tell you that....HE will tell us..his lungs will be tired his body will be tired and we will know, he will tell us with out a doubt."

There were some other things discussed I am sure that I don't recall at this moment, but the office visit that Dr. Barnes warned us about had happened.....nothing was said we hadn't already played in our heads...,but were still painful words to hear out loud. It was hard to take everything in, and I was trying to focus and make mental notes on the Dr.'s every word. Questions and thoughts running through my head, like...how hard is it going to be to say, okay, lets stop...he has been through enough, we will let Caleb be ...we will accept we have no other course...Caleb will not go through anything else, which is great...but this means we accept he will be dying....and how can that be...how can we be losing him...why isn't there anything else....something that wouldn't just prolong a life of pain, but actually stop the pain. I think these and a million other things went through my brain in .5 seconds...I snapped out of it and wouldn't allow myself to think this way anymore till, well......now. After all, we still had a blood draw, and x-ray, a feeding and a diaper change to help Caleb thru..plus, I needed to drive them both home....it was time to "buck up"!

We did the blood draw, and there was a baby in there who was being tested for Aplastic anemia..the baby boy was born April 11th, yes he was 2 days old...I quickly counted my blessings and realized Caleb was "well" for at least 3 of his 7 and 1/2 years (at least we thought and he acted like he was, we of course now know he was born with cortical dysplasia).

We left the hospital at 5:10 and Beth and Caleb were home by 7. In time for the "works"...Caleb needed food, treatments ..meds soon, diaper change...like I said the "works" and then bed around 8:30.

Beth and I talked on the way back. She and Chad will again be in need of lots of prayers as well as our little bubba and his 2 sisters.
For now, it is wait and see how soon he builds back to pneumonia...and pray hard it is a few months at least and not a few weeks.

We know this hasn't been easy to read, it wasn't easy to hear...but we appreciate each of you for taking time each time you check in on Caleb and for saying a prayer for him. We realize that this is a "downer" and I try to be uplifting on days were I can find something good or happy that Caleb did or saw

or anything to make this webpage,...well...less depressing. Tonight I am at a loss of anything good...except to say how blessed we all are and how thankful I am to have Caleb in my life everyday he is here with us. Thank You Lord for the joy Caleb has and does bring us all.
Love to all---aunt Ellen

Dealing with all of the news from that day was difficult. It makes you want to pack up and go on extended vacation, to Disney World, and to all of the other places on your list. I felt an urgency of taking him everywhere I wished he could go while he was feeling some better. And then on the other hand, he was not easily impressed by most of those things. He'd be happy or miserable, just like at home. Some days I would get in "nesting mode" to just clean the house top to bottom, or to organize. It was ridiculous, but the reason was because I felt completely out of control--because EPILEPSY was in control. I felt drawn to go to medical school, I had read enough research papers, studies, articles, abstracts on epilepsy to rival any medical library. However, there was no time for that. But, I felt with all the knowledge I'd gathered, I was unable to help my child, maybe I could continue that learning and help some other child overcome epilepsy. I am certain that doctors are able to continue their work because of those successes.

Caleb's world was full of seizures, typically around 70 to 100 a day. We were working hard to make the warm weather of the spring time to allow Caleb more time outside and with family. It seemed that our perspective on a "tough seizure day" had changed to the point that we just weren't alarmed by 100, as long as he wasn't clustering tonic seizures. But the realization that our child was terminally ill, was overshadowing our daily lives. We were consumed with his care. And the realization that he wasn't going to "get better" long term was also hard to deal with.

After all he'd been through in the past year, Chad and I decided to something we thought we'd never have to do, we prearranged our child's funeral. It was tough, overwhelming and emotional, but we made it through it. I just knew that I wanted everything set up so that when the time came, I didn't have to worry about any of the logistics or being too overwhelmed to not be able to deal with it later on. My grandfather, Bobby Peyton had been a Mortician and Funeral Service Director for many years. So, growing up with that being discussed as a normal day to day thing, made it easier in some ways, for us to consider taking that step.

I was grateful when I went home, and he was still there, resting and as comfortable as possible. And I remember praying then, that something would come along, a medication, research, a new procedure, something to prolong his life. Dr. Barnes had told us we would be very lucky to see 18. With reading all of the research I could find about children with neurological disorders, GI issues, g-tubes, fundoplications, and acquired chronic pulmonary aspiration, I was certain that our time with Caleb would be even more limited. How limited, I didn't know, but I knew I would do my best to meet every day like it was my last with him, and try to find a way to give him joy at least once a day, somehow.

Chapter 12: Swinging, Facing the Music and Seeing through the Seizures

It was May, and while it was busy for the girls with end of school activities, I was trying to make the best of Caleb's days. He always loved swinging and our local park had acquired funds from several businesses and charitable organizations, including our FEAT group (Families for Effective Autism Treatment), to build an accessible playground at the park.. It was great because some of it was wheelchair accessible and then there were wonderful special needs swings there that were wonderful for Caleb. He loved to swing. I had been given a rainy-day kit with a big net swing that hangs in a doorway and Caleb liked that, but was getting too long for it. So having somewhere to take him to swing that was safe for him was really nice.

We would usually have the place to ourselves, but occasionally there would be someone there with pre-schoolers, and they typically would ask about Caleb's chair. I would explain that his legs didn't work anymore and they were usually very interested and very sweet to Caleb. Usually kids are more accepting and open than their parents are. But, if the child starts the conversation, a child in a wheelchair can bring the biggest of people to their true "good selves".

Caleb's respiratory issues continued to be troublesome with periods of chest retraction, and wheezing. It would look like an asthma attack, however, he could recover on his own, because rather than asthma, we were dealing with aspiration. It just made me sick to see him struggling to breathe, because I was as helpless as he was. And usually right after an episode like this, a respiratory infection was right around the corner, followed by more antibiotics. It was a vicious cycle.

Mary had added more calories to his diet and finally by the end of May, he'd gained a pound! We were so glad. He was still a tall and gangly little man, but he was gaining, and that was so important. She worked in June to get him moved to whipping cream instead of powdered formula to cut out additives in his diet in hopes to reduce seizures further. It did help to calm down his myoclonics for a while, so we were grateful.

At the end of June Caleb was having another increase in seizure activity and more problems with his lungs. Dr. Moore explained that his issues with breathing were a progression of Caleb's overall deterioration, that was tough to hear. However, as a mom, you want to know what you are dealing with, and the truth is when you have a sick child, you feel in your heart where they are, and you are usually right. To have someone in a white coat to agree with you, enables you to deal with the fact medically and emotionally. I told Dr. Moore "we know we can't "fix" Caleb at this point, but we want him to be as happy and as okay as he can be." And as always, Dr. Moore let me know they would do the best they could to keep him as happy and comfortable as possible. It was a moment of change in viewing how we treated Caleb.

Before this visit, I knew where he was, but dealing with it rationally was another thing. There is always hope, and I kept praying that there was something out there that would change for him, somehow.

We saw Dr. Barnes again the end of June and did the usual "tweaking of meds". He confirmed we were in a "catch 22", meaning if his respiratory was better then seizures would improve and if seizures were improved then his respiratory would. So Dr. Barnes and Dr. Moore worked diligently together to try to give Caleb some improvement! Dr. Moore started Caleb on a Coughilator, which is a device that gives positive air in and then pulls that air out in an attempt to enable Caleb's weak lungs to cough. It worked the first time we used it! We were thrilled to have something that could improve his cough and make it more productive so we could suction it out and keep his lungs clean.

We tried Caleb at the spray park one July day, he tolerated his toe in it for a moment and then touched the water one time and then was finished, but I was glad we tried! He loved water, but some days it just wasn't his thing. The beginning of July always made me anxious, Caleb typically would have increased seizures, and he was following that pattern again this July. So I stayed in close contact with Dr. Barnes and we made adjustments as needed to try to keep up with Caleb's activity and keep us out of the hospital. Changing things and "holding on" for what would happen next had become the norm. I can remember Dr. Barnes patting Caleb on the head and quietly telling him "try not to show out and make mom a wreck this week." And if I asked him what to expect next, he would say "ask Caleb," in other words, there was no way to know. Caleb was a rare case for certain.

We finally on the home front were able to secure year round respite care and personal care workers. It took some time to get it all set up, but it was a huge help. I had a rule that I would not be away from Caleb for more than a 5 minute radius. So it was tough to get everything done in a day that needed taking care of, but with an extra set of hands, I could prepare meds and feedings for him and run to the grocery or to pay bills without having to do "drive through only errands." The days of carting him around to public places had long been over, but without extra hands the grocery store had to wait. It was also good for Nana and Ellen not to have to be at my house every day. They had families and themselves to take care of and spent plenty of time with us still, but having someone else there made it more of a visit for them instead of coming to my house to work. And they still had to fill in during hospital stays and Dr. office visits!

Excerpt from Caringbridge entry July 12, 2009- to Team Caleb

"I can't tell you what a comfort it is to write on here from time to time, but it is therapy for me, and sometimes saying/printing out what is going on with Caleb allows us to accept it, no matter how unpleasant it may be. There are times I just want to bawl my eyes out, but I can come here and give you all an update and somehow I draw strength and peace with where we are and where we're going. I have my moments, trust me, but knowing you all are there, you truly help me carry on."

Caleb would have periods of time where he wanted Mommy to hold him, and I ate that up. He would some times be able to look you straight in the eyes and it would just make you cry. It's though he was needing me to make him feel safe somehow, I would pray that he would know that if I could take his pain away I would do it in a moment.

Every day was a battle to keep him well, but we would try to fill his day with familiar people, favorite toys and videos, and strolls around the block in the sunshine. I tried to make it to worship as often as I could and on nice days or evenings, if Caleb was well enough, we would drive to church and Papa or other family members would take turns strolling Caleb outside. He enjoyed it and I could be uplifted and get a break, so it was a win/win. I still kept Caleb away from the public, so I wouldn't take him in, but our friends there would wave to him or blow him kisses!

Before school began again, we took a mini trip to Nashville without any Dr. visits to let the kids go to the zoo. Caleb had been loosing more and more of his mobility and was beginning to scoot everywhere. We went to the hotel and it was evident for the first time, he wasn't able to go to the door to protest being there. Instead, he quietly lay in the floor and played with his trucks. I can remember wishing he had the ability and the attitude to protest like he had once before when he was around 4. We had gone to a hotel and he was not happy about it and went to the door. When we redirected him, he went to the window and seeing the American flag outside, started reciting the "Pledge of Allegiance" through tears, he was the saddest little thing and he was reciting it no doubt for comfort, because he couldn't express his needs to us. I remember we took him for a swim right after that, which cheered him up at the time!

We started Caleb on a new AED (Anti-epileptic drug) called Banzel on August 4th. We were hoping for improvement. We were praying for even a little bit of a break from the normal 100 seizures a day.

Caringbridge entry: Tuesday August 4th, 2009

Team Caleb,
Hi, Caleb has had a rough few days, he's just been worn out, and his sleep patterns are crazy. He is waking up during the night around 3 and staying awake for a couple of hours, then when he goes back to sleep, he'll have a huge tonic seizure. So our schedule for him has been off too.

We have been working to get him off of Clobazam so we can try something else, there are a couple of new seizure meds that just came out this spring, so today we get to start a new one. It's called "Banzel" and it can help children with Lennox-Gastaut : a type of syndrome of Epilepsy. Caleb doesn't have this type, however, some of his seizures have similar patterns. So it may help, SO WE ARE GIVING IT A TRY!

At least there are drugs out there being researched and developed to try to help these kids. We are so blessed to live in a country that (at least for now) that has the best funding for

research in new medications, without them, there would be nothing left to try, so we are grateful.

We are also so lucky to have Team Caleb at Vandy. Dr. Barnes, Mary Montgomery, Dr. Pearson, Dr. Moore and our nurse Ginny are just amazing. They truly care so much. Dr. Barnes had emailed me about giving it a try and before I even received his email, Ginny had me on the phone telling me side effects, what to watch for and dosage instructions. There is nothing like Vanderbilt, it is simply AMAZING. WE LOVE YOU!!!!

Please pray for this new medicine to help Caleb. He so deserves a break from seizures.

He has been showing a bit more "attitude" about what is on TV. So that is always good to see that at least he cares!!! He can't tell us, but he'll grab the DVD player , so you know some things can really be said without words!!!

He also really looked at me right in the eyes last night, and smiled, now that's something that I'd pay all the money in the world for. Of course when he did I talked for him and said "Hi Mama, I love you." And he still smiled, and I told him "Mama loves Caleb." and he smiled, and I will live on that for a long time, it is priceless and it lets me know, my Caleb is still there even with all the seizures, with the struggles of walking, and breathing, and sensory issues and autism, some times Caleb just breaks through all of that, and his eyes are clear, and they just melt your heart and we become more determined to keep

up the fight.
I love you all.
Beth

Chapter 13: Changes, Regression and Hope

GI issues and retching continued and we tried smaller amounts and more frequent bolus feedings to try to help with that. Caleb continued having GI issues and constipation built up so that an enema at home wouldn't work. We had to take him to Vandy for a Milk and Molasses Enema, and with that said, I will tell you that as bad as that sounds, it is, and I will leave it at that. Caleb was in pain, and it was awful. However, the retching continued and it was evident that Caleb needed continual feeding in order for him to receive his feeds slowly and allow his body to tolerate it.

We also starting seeing a GI specialist, Dr. Anderson. She added Nexium and Zofran to his meds to help with nausea and to help his feeds settle. And we added mirolax to his schedule to help with motility. We also worked with Mary on getting his water in him slowly. The problem seemed to be too much volume in his stomach, so we were doing small bits at a time every hour.

Within a week after this change, Caleb's seizures were increasing again, and the thought that his GI was now deteriorating was devastating to deal with. However, it was evident that he needed a change to help him. He also cried continually and it was tearing my heart. We were increasing meds to try to keep up with the seizures and at the same time watching for respiratory illness, and now dealing with a bag attached to him 20 hours a day that we had to keep in a backpack so he could try to be as mobile as he could. It was an adjustment.

One evening, during a violent tonic his hand was holding onto his feed line and he pulled his Mic-key button out, it was not good. I had not officially changed one before, and this 3 am tonic and catastrophe was not my ideal timing on figuring out how to do it, but with Chad's help holding him I managed to get it done, while he continued to have repetitive tonics. It was just sad.

We went to see Dr. Barnes again and Mary for more "tweaking" in September. The Banzel was helping reduce the number of myoclonics that he was having daily, and we were cautiously optimistic. It was nice to be a bit more stable for once in the seizure department, he was still having them daily, but overall 60-100 daily was better than 100+. He was also more stable in the pulmonary area, so it was a good start before the germs started coming home from school with the girls.

Then October brought the typical viral throat infections for the girls and for Caleb too. We did our best to "scrub them in" when they came home, but we couldn't block everything. He developed a rash and I was worried at first it was from the Banzel (a bad side effect), however, it turned out to be viral. So, we found a glycerin free steroid cream to use on it to clear it up thanks to Dr. Mudd, and we were glad when it cleared.

Caleb's tonic seizures continued to worsen. We were trying to wean Felbatol down a bit as we were increasing the Banzel. But, it just wasn't going to work. The key as Dr. Barnes always explained was the smallest amount of AED's we could get away with, with optimal performance was the goal. However, with

Caleb, it seemed as though the higher levels of everything was where we would end up to keep us out of the ER. Every bit of a reduction required an increase somewhere else, and many times we would be unable to reduce the AED at all, with Felbatol this was the case.

Later in October, another sinus infection hit, so another round of antibiotics. I was doing his respiratory therapy every 6 hours around the clock as always, so we just kept it up to try to keep him clear.

Also, we got a packet in the mail from Make-A-Wish. They were going to grant Caleb a wish! We were so excited for him, and at that same moment, the realization of where your child is, just came crashing down on me at the same time. I wished he was able to talk, or in some way to communicate to us what he'd like to do. He was losing more and more of his mobility, many times crawling and his little arms just giving way. So the things that made him happy were little things, trucks, boxes, Barney videos and comforting hugs. So we just prayed for more stability, and that we would be able to pick something for him to do that would bring him some joy.

The tonic seizures were up to 25 to 30 a day, which was not normal, and I spent many nights being awakened by Caleb seizing. It was harder on him during the day too, when he would have these larger tonics while awake. They just weren't giving up despite our best efforts, but we were determined not to give up either.

In November we celebrated another birthday on November 7th, with our sweet boy.

Caringbridge entry: Friday, November 6th:

Team Caleb,

Thank you all for your cards and gifts sent to Caleb. It means so much! We are all blessed to have friends across the country who love our little guy and continue to lift him up in prayer daily.

I am so grateful to have our Caleb in our lives. I can't believe he's already 8 years old. Time sure flies. He has been through so much.

He's been the typical into everything toddler, to the child that we couldn't discipline, that didn't understand us, that was screaming for help to communicate, to diagnosed with Autism. He went through therapies, Dietary, Occupational, Physical, Speech, Water, Behavioral, and Educational, and made great strides, he made sentences, like "I love you Mommy." and "Zeb play with me" and "Daddy I need juice box."

Then the seizures came and things learned started to slip away. His words became fewer. He struggled to communicate. We used cards and objects. We started a new diet, the Ketogenic, and his teachers were so good with him. They counted the

number of pepperonis he ate in a day so I could calculate everything at home. He has been on over 12 different kinds of anticonvulsants. He has lost his speech altogether. He can't grab cards. He rarely walks. He seizes incessantly.

But he can communicate with a look, he can make you smile and warm your heart when he laughs at a familiar show or song. He is patient. He is content with the smallest of things. He is always a good listener. He likes peace and calm and order. He expects you to anticipate his needs. He will let you know when he doesn't want you to read to him. He will listen to you sing, and lets you know when to stop.

He is loving. He snuggles. He looks to us for comfort. He looks to us for help. He looks in your eyes sometimes, and you can see the soul of an angel. There are so many things lost. But with those things gone, the simple things are appreciated all the more.

Every birthday is a blessing to every child, but for Caleb, those birthdays are milestones of another year of triumph. And the start of another year, to hope and pray for something to ease the seizures and allow him to truly have peace.

Caleb,
I am so blessed to be your Mommy. I love you with all my heart. You cannot read this, but I know that you know I love you. You are the strongest child I know. You make me a better person. I am grateful to God for you and for all you are. I am

proud of how you deal with tough days, and for how you fight on. Don't give up. Happy 8th birthday Baby boy. You are my hero. I love you, Mommy

**Love to all of you,
Beth**

Caleb's December started off with another sinus infection which precipitated long tonic seizures and retching. He was placed on antibiotics again, this time for 21 days to try to help him clear the infection. We consulted with all of Caleb's specialists and they recommended changes here and there to try to help him through. He had also lost weight again. After running some blood work it was found that his Carnitine level was low, which is needed to absorb fats. Mary quickly got Carnitine replacement medication ordered, and we hoped that would help him "regain" some weight. We also started Topamax for the clustering of tonics during Caleb's sleep that were unrelenting. I was concerned it would make him lethargic, but with all of the other medications he was on, it didn't seem to make much of a difference.

Seizure Log Caleb Baker 2009

Month	myoclonic	tonic	totals
Jan.	1948	243	2318
Feb.	1671	360	2038
Mar.	2637	369	3011
Apr.	2221	401	2663
May.	2143	567	2722
Jun.	2505	453	2975
Jul.	2922	482	3498
Aug.	2203	496	3114
Sept.	1446	209	1998
Oct.	1200	432	1684
Nov.	1245	433	1702
Dec.	862	525	1393

The start of a new year always brings hopes. We had lots of hopes for Caleb, that we knew were not realistic, so we settled with the goal of keeping him as happy as possible. The sweet people from Make-A-Wish came to visit us. Chad and I thought long and hard about what the best opportunity out there would be for Caleb. We considered a hot tub, which he would have enjoyed. However, our home was not equipped to house a hot tub. We decided on a trip to Florida, and the volunteers from MAW told us about Give Kids The World. It sounded wonderful, and we were so glad a place like this existed for families of terminally ill children. The bonus was, Caleb would get to meet Barney, his favorite pal, his comforter, his happiness. We were happy for him, although, he couldn't understand to anticipate it, we knew it would make him happy!

We dealt with more issues of aspiration and drops in Caleb's oxygen levels in early January. Which resulted in an ER run. We were told that this continual esophageal relaxation was the problem by Pulmonology. So, Dr. Barnes was trying to wean Caleb from Felbatol again to try to see if he could do without as much and that it in turn might regain him more control over involuntary processes. He also had problems of continual retching. The decision was made by GI to place Caleb's G-tube into his jejunum (the opening to his small intestine). This GJ procedure could be done by Interventional Radiology at Vandy. We had it done on January 19th, 2010. We had been combating the constant retching with Nexium and Zofran, but it was not helping. We were concerned that with all the retching going on, there would be the possibility of Caleb's fundoplication opening up. This would require surgery to repair, so that was something we were hoping to avoid. So we were very hopeful that the GJ placement would help.

Unfortunately, bouts of retching continued. We increased his Zofran dosage and were careful to give him this an hour before his medications were due. It seemed that this change was helping some. We were beginning to become overwhelmed with the new med schedule. His last meds for the night were at 11 pm and we were giving him his first round at 5 am. I stayed up to do his 11's and then Chad would get up every morning and do the 5's so that I wouldn't have to wake for those. However, now Caleb's sleep was worsening as well. He would wake at 3 in the morning and be a nervous wreck until about 6 and then have a large tonic, and fall back asleep, and have many myoclonic seizures. It was exhausting for him.

The seizures progressed and we had to put the Felbatol back where it was. It was just clearly helping too much to risk taking him off of it. We also dealt with more respiratory issues, and a viral GI infection in February. But, we were able again with "Team Caleb at Vandy," to help him through.

The first of March we were back at Vandy for routine check-ups with Dr. Moore in Pulmonology and Dr. Barnes in Neurology. They were wonderful at coordinating our appointments. We were in the waiting room before our Neurology appointment. Caleb went into a huge tonic seizure. I used to worry if others around would be upset by what they saw, just not wanting them to be upset. Sadly, seeing seizures every day almost made us numb to them, but the tonic seizures, I don't care how many he had daily, I never got "used to them". I don't know how you could. It is just heartbreaking, every single time.

He also had problems with meds coming up into his J tube that we saw when a connector on his feed line had popped open. We were concerned that the J had backed up into his G, but after our Neuro appointment we took him to Radiology and the J was in place. They told us that sometimes there is reflux in the stomach that moves through the flap that hangs open where the J tube to the small intestine is.

We were trying all we could to get the retching to stop, but now the fact that his AED's, the meds he needed the most could be seeping out of his stomach too quickly for them to be absorbed as needed and going into his J was troublesome. There was nothing that could be done.

Caringbridge entry: Thursday March 11th, 2010

Team Caleb,
Met with Dr. Mudd yesterday, he checked him over and agreed he's not ill and has no signs of infection. I caught him up on all that's been going on the last couple of months.
We discussed what all were "possibilities" of the latest GI issues. I and he agree that most likely this is just the progress of Caleb's condition. Dr. Mudd said, "this is the part where, I'm not going to cry and you're not going to cry...but I have to say, this is just Caleb and we love him and we're going to take care of him, but this is just where he is." I can't tell you how much I appreciate him, and his honesty at letting me know

when we are going through another stage of "loss". I told him I'd cried about it last week, so this week I am ready to deal with wherever he is and try to help "manage" whatever is going on so he is as comfortable as he can be.

I will be glad to see Dr. Anderson and let her decide what can be done to manage the weight loss and absorption issues. I got an email from Vandy and one GI doctor doesn't have a spot open for the scope...which Dr. Anderson may/may not decide to do.

The blood work from yesterday has come back fine, his glucose was a bit low, but that's from his diet. So liver issues are not the cause, neither is pancreas, or other enzyme/chemical related issues. So that leaves malabsorption and from what research I've done...that is typical with Neurologically Impaired children.

So we're going to do what a special teacher advised me years ago, and "meet him where he is, every day." We never know where that is going to be, some are fantastic and some are terrible, but wherever and whatever we are dealing with, we are not alone.

I watched a great movie last night with Caleb, and a quote from it seemed to really just fit our day.." the truth of God's love is not that He allows bad things to happen, it's His promise that He'll be there with us when they do." Every step along this journey we have been blessed to have God here to strengthen us and be able to deal with where Caleb is.

Thank you all for your continued love and prayers, we love you all,
Beth

GI issues continued. Caleb would lay on his belly during the day and when he slept, which he had never done before. We had an appointment with Dr. Anderson in GI on March 22nd and along with Mary Montgomery, developed a plan. We started him on Flagyl, suspecting an infection from his constant need for antibiotics. We also started him on VSL #3, a super powered probiotic to try to promote good bacteria in his gut. We also began a regular scheduled venting of his GJ. And we added more calories to try to combat his weight loss.

The next morning, Caleb woke me at 3 am struggling to breathe. His oxygen level had dropped to 88. I made some calls, Caleb spiked a fever, and we took him to the ER at Vanderbilt Children's. We had an x-ray, which showed the typical "Caleb cloudiness". All the staff "Team Caleb" at Vandy knew we were there and a parade of visitors began. Caleb was lethargic and pitiful. His seizures continued. I asked for a stool sample to be done after he had a terrible episode of diarrhea. Two days later the answer came back: Clostidium Difficile or C Diff. It is an infection of the gut that kills out good bacteria, typically from use of lots of antibiotics. This disease attacks the colon and is highly contagious. So all diapers from that point on were changed while "gloved up." His poor little belly just had to be worn out. Our attending doctor said she was realizing that everything with Caleb was a "catch 22." I asked for a plan before we headed home, since we were 1 week away from taking Caleb on his Make-A-Wish trip.

We increased his respiratory treatments, his coughilator treatments and he was on Bactrum. His med schedule was even more crazy, and I had to get them all redone just so I could think through what would need to be done, but we managed it. Aunt Ellen was a blessing to have with us to help us through another hospitalization. Chad and Nana held down the home front schedules for the girls. We were glad to be home.

We touched base with Dr. Mudd before leaving for the trip to Florida. He saw, for the first time, Caleb go into a tonic seizure. He was bothered by it, as we always were. Just the fact that the short time we were there with him he could see Caleb seize bothered me. He just wasn't as well as I had hoped he would be for the trip. But, there was no promise of an improvement from where he was, so I felt like we needed to get him as well as possible and let him see Barney!

Chapter 14: Making Memories and Managing Care

We left on Friday, April 2nd. We drove to Nashville and got ready for an early morning flight. On Saturday we reached Orlando. We had to take the Coughilator with us since there wasn't one in all of Florida they could get for us! But the staff on the plane were great about helping us with it and we made it there with all of our luggage and equipment. At one point, I looked up from the screening room for Caleb since he was in his wheelchair, and there Chad stood in a sea of luggage!! But we made it!

Give Kids The World was the most wonderful place. Everyone there had children with debilitating diseases or terminal illnesses. There was no staring or questionable looks, because we were all in the same circumstances. It was a place of acceptance. It also was a place where we were treated like royalty from the moment we arrived. There were accessible activities for Caleb that we could all enjoy with him. There were gifts and activities and tickets to all the theme parks and to several other attractions. We knew Caleb would not be up to long days. So we scheduled one thing to do each day and just hoped he would feel good enough to be able to go. He was able to enjoy Sea World, he loved the big TV's at the Shamoo show, but his absolute favorite were the penguins..he was entranced! Then the next day we took him to Universal Studios where he met his lifelong comforter- BARNEY!!
We went to the Barney land, there was a store, so we looked for any Barney video that Caleb didn't have- but we had them all! So we got him a big stuffed Barney and a Barney t-shirt. We then went to the Barney show. It was precious. His eyes went directly

to that stage and he watched intently as Barney, BJ and Baby Bop danced around the stage and sang his favorite songs. At the end, they sang the "I love you" song, Chad and I both broke down in tears! Afterward, the staff asked us to stay. Barney came out and met Caleb personally and got pictures made with us. Caleb was fascinated by his big feet and wanted to grab his toes! It was precious.

The next day we went to Magic Kingdom and we rode all of Caleb's favorite rides from when we had went when he was 4. We rode Peter Pan's flight about 5 times! We also did "It's a Small World" and he loved the little Irish man dancing. He met several characters and had a break in the middle of the day at a room for Wish Kids at Magic Kingdom. It was great because we could do a breathing treatment, let him roll around out of his wheelchair and just desensitize from the mornings activities. We stayed there for a couple of hours! Then we watched the Spectromagic parade. He absolutely loved the lights! We were next to several other families with children with special needs. A dad next to us was trying to talk his child with Autism through it because the music was so loud. I had come prepared with ear plugs just in case for that very reason, and I was glad to give them a pair, so he made it through. Caleb did fine with it but was tired, so we didn't stay for the fireworks.

The next day we had planned to see MGM Studios, and we finally got there after a tough morning getting Caleb to wake. We went to The Little Mermaid show, and Playhouse Disney, and he loved them! However, right after that he was back asleep. I felt like something was not right. I hated for the girls to be disappointed but they were okay with going back to the Give Kids the World village for the day and we headed to the car.

All I can say at this point was, Caleb had the worse explosion of C Diff diarrhea I have ever witnessed. I went to lift him out of his wheelchair to place him in the car and it flooded him, the wheelchair, the parking lot, everything. I called for help from the girls and Chad. We managed to find some plastic bags and Camille started handing me wipes. Chad was digging for more clothes and Peyton grabbed a "chuck" (a bed pad) that we always had with us for messy changes. I asked for Chad to hold Caleb under his arms while I tried to undress him. Peyton was holding the chuck up as a modesty partition. Camille was handing me wipes and I was slathering off the ooze headed down his legs when he started seizing. I about had an all out meltdown. But then, I looked up and I saw Camille readying another wipe, dodging the diarrhea all around her in puddles. I saw Peyton standing there trying to keep onlookers from seeing the battlefield. And Chad holding him while he seized. There was nothing to do but go on, clean it up, and try to help Caleb. After his clothes were bagged and thrown away we got him into his carseat, with nothing but his diaper on. Chad and I were shoeless and blotched with C Diff on our clothes. We cleaned up the wheelchair as best as we could, and the parking lot. Every wipe we had with us was put to maximum use! The girls crawled in the car and comforted Caleb, who finally quit seizing. We got to the village and after 3 more hours of clean up and showers, we were C Diff free--except for our sweet boy, who was still dealing with this terrible illness in his gut.

It was heartbreaking.

We called Vandy for more meds and another round of Flagyl was called in to a pharmacy there so we could get Caleb some help. We were grateful.

The girls were so good to him and were content with doing whatever he was able to do and not complaining about what they couldn't. They didn't ride one thing that Caleb was not able/would not like. They were diligent in helping us get through the C Diff nightmare. We were so proud of them. They got some extra pool time in at GKTW. Caleb rested the rest of Wednesday and Thursday we went for an hour to Epcot and let the girls buy some souvenirs. We also let Caleb ride Soarin' and he loved it, he even smiled!!! It was a blessing to see that! Friday we got to meet Barney again at GKTW and have our picture taken with him in the castle. And then we flew home.

It was a great trip, and we were so thankful to Make-A-Wish and Give Kids The World for a wonderful week of sweet memories. There were clearly some rough patches on the trip, but every week was like that. It was great to be able to have the community of people there to help us make the most of every moment, that after all is what life is all about.

Caleb's condition continued to exasperate once we got home. He began running a temperature. His lungs didn't sound good and his seizures were increasing.

After two rounds of DiaStat to try and stop clustering of tonic seizures, (they were happening every 2 minutes), I loaded Caleb up and took him to Vandy ER, again. They went over all the medications he was on and all the medications for seizures that he had been on in the past and then asked, "what do you think would work." So I asked for a load of Dilantin, and they came and gave it to him. It worked as usual in slowing them. So I was grateful.
He continued to be lethargic and experience retching.

Monday April 19th, 2010 Caringbridge entry:

Team Caleb~~~

Caleb has been retching a lot since yesterday. He has also become lethargic.

The Neuro team came in this morning along with Mary.

So far, they are changing the VNS and adjusting it up a little so that when Beth swipes him, it might help some.
Mary is reducing the oil ratio amounts to see if that will help the retching....the bad thing is it will probably increase his myoclonic activity. They have also sent a GI consult to see what changes they could suggest.

They drew a dylantin blood panel to see how much is still in his system, they think that could be causing the lethargy.

Here's Beth's take. She thinks Caleb is not well. This has been

typical of his "I'm sick " pattern of late....lethargy added with retching. Something is up...and it may be a few days till they figure it out. She doesn't suspect this is simply a Neuro-medication change that is needed.

That's all the news I received this morning. I will post more as I get it. (AKA, Nana, call me with some info!)
Please continue to pray for Caleb, for the Dr's. to figure out what his latest battle is quickly, and for there to be a non-invasive treatment.Love to all~
Aunt Ellen

Tuesday April 20th, 2010 Caringbridge entry:

Team Caleb~~~

Well, Caleb is home. He was released this afternoon, not to Beth's liking, but never the less....

He was back on his feeds bag, and so far was/is doing okay, no retching. My understanding is that the dietitian (our dear friend Mary) was wanting to keep Caleb till tomorrow to make sure he could keep his feeds down without retching. Evidently that theory got lost in translation, or was ignored and the Floor Dr. took charge and had him released. Beth was on her BEST behavior, and so, she allowed it....although she made sure everyone knew how she felt about it.

All I can say is, I SURE hope he keeps from retching

tonight,..or heads will roll. LOL!

Anyone who knows Beth knows she will not tolerate being pushed around...especially when it comes to her babies...so we will see how this all plays out.

The important thing is, for now the big Tonic seizures are staying away. The myoclonics have picked up, which we figured would happen, just not this soon already.

I think sis just hates that Caleb is at a place now where he doesn't go home from the hospital 'any better' than he went in as far as overall condition. Yes, they stopped the big seizures. But there was no..."new plan" of how to help him from now on. and that has to hurt any mother. There is just a "if he gets this bad...take him in, treat the symptoms and carry your son back home." Its tough to do that willingly. In this day and age, we think there should/has to be a medical answer for every problem. Sometimes there is....huge advances have kept Caleb with us for this long. Then there are times when there is nothing new out there to try.

We never heard the theory on WHY he had this sporadic increase in seizures this weekend....I'm uncertain there are answers for why on many questions.

We know this, Caleb is home, and he is resting. Should tomorrow come for all of us, it will be the day which the Lord has made and we should be glad and rejoice in it. Ps. 118:24

**Thank you all for your prayers. Love to all~~~
Aunt Ellen**

200 seizures a day were the new norm. It was not a welcome sight. However the increases in AED's were keeping us out of the ER once again.

On the GI front, we started Reglan, a last resort motility drug to try to keep things moving in his gut. We also scheduled an endoscopy to make sure there were no blockages. Which turned out fine.

For respiratory, we started inhaled antibiotics of Tobrimycin. This was a tremendous help and most importantly, kept Caleb's lungs clear without tearing up his GI like other oral antibiotics had been. I was so glad when we started finally seeing some improvement at home with the use of the Tobi. I knew Caleb had to at least feel some better in this department, now to fight the GI and seizures!!!

Chapter 15: Blessings of Family

On a pretty day in May, we were able to get Caleb out to the park to swing in the special needs swings. Our family, Chad, me, Peyton, Camille and Caleb went. It was nice just to spend time "just us," as usually there were at least one or two other helpers at home with us every day. We needed them, but it made home life very different than for most people. We were so grateful to have help, but in that same turn, we wished we were able to be a more independent of all the meds, bags, equipment, nurses, therapists, and respite team that was a part of our everyday now. However, it kept Caleb going, so it was a necessity.

When we left Give Kids The World, they gave us a "Passport" that gave us free tickets to various parks across the country. We were hoping to get Caleb well enough that we could take him a couple of places. So in May, we went to Holiday World with a big group of family and friends. There wasn't a lot that Caleb could do, but we managed to get him on the carousel and train. He also liked putting his hands in the fountains. It was a nice day, so he was comfortable and we were able to stroll him around everywhere, so he liked that.

Going anywhere, from an afternoon at Nana's to a trip to Florida took the same amount of luggage: Feed bags, formula, IV pole for feed bag, replacement bags, replacement tubes, emergency replacement mic-key button, thermometers, stethoscope, O2 monitor, coughilator, nebulizer, suction machine and tubes, all his meds, mortar and pestle for grinding the meds, water, and usually 3 changes of clothes, diapers, wipes, chucks and toys. It wasn't a light load. But it was important for him to go as much as possible to make experiences and try to have moments of happiness for him. So we went.

Aunt Ellen was lovingly called "the pack mule", because she was with us for most of our Dr. visits, hospitalizations, afternoon excursions, etc.

Excerpt from Caringbridge entry : Thursday May, 6, 2010

" just wanted to tell you all how fortunate we are to have an Aunt Ellen in our family. I am blessed more than I can say to have such a loving/giving family. My sister is the absolute best there is. She makes time to help me carry a load no matter what is going on in her life. She and Zeb can pack and be ready to roll in warp speed. She has missed out on time with Zeb, crucial hours that could have been spent at home taking care of her family, when she was helping me through some of the worst days I've ever experienced. Her being with me allows Chad to continue to work, which we desperately need him to do. It lets Peyton and Camille have at least one parent at home while I'm away. It lets me have peace of mind that the rest of our family is back home to help navigate all that needs taking care of. And most of all, she is the friend I need when some times have been really tough. She's gone through IV's, surgeries, seizure meds, EEG's, G-tubes, J-tubes, VNS's, fundoplications, Caleb going into Status and both of us praying to keep him safe while he seized in our arms uncontrollably in

the ER, and even Milk and Molasses enemas. Most people don't dream up some of this stuff, but she's gone through it all with me. I only hope that some day I can help her as much as she has helped me, and I pray that my girls will be as good friends/sisters to each other as we are blessed to be. Love you Aunt Ellen."

Caleb's seizures continued and we continued to try to combat them with increases in his Topamax. The brain is an amazing design of God, and it is amazing how adaptive it really is to all the things we tried to do to stop the seizures. But, when "normal" is seizing, I guess it make sense that no matter what you do, his brain adjusts to it all and goes back to his seizures. It was an unending battle.

Pretty summer days brought Caleb lots of trips around the neighborhood on his golf cart, and he enjoyed it. His little hands would be crammed in his mouth, but he would relax a little bit from time to time, and he would seem pretty content. When he was finished and wanted to go in the house he would flail his legs or grab your arm and we'd take him back to the house.

Caleb's nervousness increased, his tonics increased, we increased his meds, the cycle continued. Caleb began pinching incessantly his clothes with one hand and the other he kept in his mouth. He rarely would grab a toy, just needed his hands more for pinching and mouthing…it was sad. He was very adamant on not wanting to walk. But occasionally if we tried, to "walk" him through the house, he would pat the front door, so we'd take him for a ride, and it would calm him some.

The realization that the small regressions, a little lost a little at a time, were actually a blessing sank in. Sometimes what we had to do to keep him "okay" daily was overwhelming. But, we didn't start out doing all of it. He had deteriorated in baby steps backward, so that I could be able to get used to the "new thing" and could get adjusted to it before we'd move on to another loss or another medication or another procedure.

August was a busy month with appointments. We were holding steady in the respiratory and GI departments. And when we met with Dr. Barnes he asked "Caleb, you just want to keep us on our toes and make sure we're working hard don't ya?" And that was the truth! He always seemed to be a step ahead of us and we decided to be more aggressive with his meds to try to bring him back down to a normal range of seizures. I felt like we were still setting on the "bubble" that was getting ready to burst. And I was determined to avoid the hospital if at all possible.

Aunt Ellen, and some friends of ours Rachel and Anthony Wallace who ran lawnmower derbys, put together a fundraiser for Caleb called "Crashing for Caleb," in August. It was a very hot day, but we took our golf cart up to the event so we could ride Caleb around and make a breeze for him! There were over 300 people there, reporters, derby folks, Peyton's LOMS Beta Club group, many friends and many family. It was a wonderful day. They raised enough money for us to pay off Caleb's PET Scan from back in "08, and to put funds aside for our frequent trips to Nashville and for extra expenses that insurance didn't cover. We were so blessed and overwhelmed by the love we felt that day.

On August 24th, 2010 we took Caleb to meet some lifelong friends who also made him very happy, "The Wiggles!" They were in Nashville and I told Chad we needed to take him if he could stay well enough, so we bought tickets back in June and we were thankful he was well enough to go! He really enjoyed it and even smiled a couple of times, it was priceless. This was the first time I could think of that just Chad and I and Caleb had done anything together, just for Caleb, without the girls. We got him a t-shirt and a cute little light up "Big Red Car".

We worked through September in clearing his "Darth Vader" sounding chest with another round of Tobi. We were thankful that inhaled antibiotics existed and that his lungs could improve over a couple of weeks. He was very tired most of the time. But after having over 4000 seizures in August, who wouldn't be?! Bless him.

Sample of :Caleb's Schedule 8/18/10
5am- zofran 10mls water

6 am -meds/76ml water (see 1pm note)

8am-breathing treatment - atrovent and pulmicort plus coughilator 5 reps; break for 3; 5 reps at 30/30 pressure

8 am- 76ml water DISCONNECT CONTINUAL FEEDS

10 am -76 ml water

11am- 76ml water with zofran plus Reglan
12 pm -2.5 mg melatonin and topamax in 25mls water
RECONNECT CONTINUAL FEEDS; 47 mls per hour for 22 hours
12:00- breathing treatment- atrovent and coughilator
Nap

1pm -meds 76 ml water (whatever needed water to mix meds subtract from 76 to get amount of water left)

3pm- 76 ml water

4pm 2mls Reglan and 25mls water

5pm - 76 ml water with 1 cap mirolax

6pm- 25mls water with topamax

7pm - 76ml water and zofran

9 pm -meds-76ml water
Breathing treatment- pulmicort and atrovent plus coughilator 5 reps;break for 3; 5 reps

12pm- 25 mls water with topamax
(This is a listing of Caleb's feeding and water schedule and his

respiratory schedule, some of his meds are listed when there were just 1 in the doseage, most of the time where "meds" are noted, Caleb was receiving multiple medications at once that were grinded together and administered)

But, by the end of September, in just one week he had over 2600, so again, we started playing "catch up." We added another AED, called Vimpat and increased his Felbatol to see if that would help, it did short term, but we were happy for any improvement. We were doing blood work as well to monitor his levels and make sure things were okay, and they came back fine.

He stabilized enough, that for Fall Break we got away for a few days with our family and Ellen, Jason and Zeb to Gatlinburg. The weather was wonderful. My brother David and his wife Elizabeth and Norah came up that way too and it was nice to be with them. We took our GKTW Passport and went to the aquarium there, Caleb really enjoyed it. He always loved looking at the fish, and it was quiet and peaceful.

Just being able to get away for a few days was a workout, but we felt it was necessary to do as much as we could with Caleb while we could. Finding things to do that he could be happy with were difficult, but he loved the car ride and enjoyed the calm of the aquarium, and that alone was worth all the effort to make it happen. Time with our family was a blessing.

Chapter 16: Giving Him Back to God

October brought illness to the girls, and we worked hard to get them better, and we were "scrubbing in" at home and keeping them isolated to their rooms in hopes to keep Caleb well. However strong our attempts, we failed and he developed the same infection, cough, fever, and crud, so he had to be started on antibiotics again. I was fearful of his GI issues, and prayed we'd get past it without C Diff reoccurring. We put him back on the "Cadillac" probiotic VSL#3 to try to ward off the bad and increase the good, at Mary Montgomery's recommendation.

October 20th, 2010, after a severe increase in seizures which would not respond to DiaStat and complete lethargy, we took Caleb to our local hospital, where they loaded him with Dilantin, did some blood work and came back with an even worse answer. Caleb had Aplastic Anemia. While this was something we knew we might deal with because of him being on Felbatol, he had been on it for over 2 years, so we thought we were "out of the woods" so to speak. We were transferred by ambulance to Vanderbilt Children's and were met by some familiar faces, but also a whole new set of doctors who spoke the language of Hematology, an area I was not able to interpret well, yet. The consensus was to do a bone marrow biopsy to see what was going on. The best of the best took him back to do the procedure. It was minimally invasive, but still troubling that we were being faced with another issue to try to overcome.

The results were that his cells were damaged but not depleted.

They recommended us to stop using Felbatol. This was a serious issue, as it had been helping, some. So reluctantly, we gave it up, to be replaced with our hospital ER drug, Dilantin, as a new part of Caleb's daily regimen. This was a huge blow. While going through the transition Caleb had over 700 seizures in a 24 hour period. The Neurology Team asked to plug him into another Video EEG. While I felt it completely unnecessary at this point, if it would give them any inkling of an idea on how to help, we had to allow it.

However, after the EEG, there was one clear conclusion. Little if anything would help.

Deep down I knew this, but to hear it from the Chief of Neurology, just reaffirmed the inevitable.

Dr. Barnes and Mary both called and came by several times. And we gathered up a plan to get him home. Although, this time going home sick with him, we would be dealing with GI, respiratory, Neurology, and Hematology now. We went for weekly blood draws hoping that somehow his white blood cells and red blood cells would increase. However, instead they trickled downward and his RBC's were now changing shape. In my research about Felbatol, I found that the longest period of time someone had gone on Felbatol and contracted Aplastic Anemia was a little over a year. There were furthermore no reports of a child ever having contracted Aplastic Anemia from use of Felbatol. I was not convinced that this was the answer.

We met with hematology again. I clearly had greater concern than the fellow in with us had answers, so he brought in the attending who was excellent. He "got real" with me and let me know that he too was not convinced that Felbatol was the culprit either. He told me they could make Caleb's numbers go up, but they would not stay there. There was a transfusion that could be done to boost RBC's and a drug called Neupogen that could boost the WBC's. However, he also mentioned that there was some "ugly stuff out there." From my experience at Vandy, I have never been told anything might be a possibility without a great deal of certainty that it was in fact what we were dealing with. The words "Myelodysplastic Syndrome" came from the doctor as a possibility. I had been reading about it, I knew then, that I felt like that was what we were up against.

Myelodysplastic Syndrome is a group of disorders caused by dysfunctional blood cells, specifically in the bone marrow. There is no cure. Some people can live with it for a long time. Others don't last very long. It was gut wrenching. I was praying I was wrong. I was hoping for the best, but being a realist, I knew that there was likely the case that this terrible disease was truly the new battle.

Trying to keep Caleb well was becoming a serious battle as well. He was Neutropenic, meaning that he had nothing he would be able to fight off on his own, he was making no immune fighting WBC's. It was important to do "reverse isolation" with him. We did this by wearing gloves, thorough hand washings, changing our clothes if we had been out of the house, gowning up visitors (typically only family in at this point) and at the slightest possibility of an illness- we masked up when close to him as well. If he had to go for a blood draw, he was masked. We thought that masking him might be difficult, since he really wanted his hands in his mouth when awake most of the time. But he was so tired all of the time, he didn't even care, and it was just sad. I wanted him to care and to rip that mask off like he had done so many times before, but he just closed his eyes and lay his head back, and slept.

November 7th was his 9th birthday. I was so glad that we had him with us for another year of celebration that we had made it to 9. He slept through most of his party. He aspirated several times and choked. We tried to make it fun for the other children there to help us celebrate. It was hard for me to deal with how sick Caleb was every day, but when you see healthy happy children around him, it makes it all that more obvious of how bad he really was doing. He was 9, and he couldn't eat the cake, blow out the candles or open his presents. But one thing I knew he could do every birthday, he could feel the love of all of those around him, and he could know that he means so much to all of us.

Caleb's blood cell counts remained low. And Hematology kept running blood work and tests. Caleb's lips were fragile and constantly dry and would peel and bleed. He was lethargic, all day. He did not attempt to move, but would lay wherever we put him. So we would rotate between the bed, his beloved "TV couch" and the floor. Papa brought him a super long soft pillow and we would prop him on that and he seemed to enjoy it. His belly was bothering him and he would cry in pain any time we put anything into his G-tube. We consulted with Dr. Anderson. We were dealing with more C Diff, and that can cause pain, so he was placed on more flagyl to try to help with that.

We saw Dr. Barnes for a routine check. I let him know that Caleb was basically seizing continuously throughout the night. He always had, but at this point it would wake me when he would seize. In the delirium of continually sleep deprived nights, I know I missed some. I would dream of counting seizures, I would dream that a tonic would wake me, and then I would truly wake and Caleb would be seizing. It was terrible.

He looked over Caleb's chart and I could tell he was deeply concerned about Caleb's overall health at this point. The gravity of the situation was written all over his and Mary's faces. He shared that hematology also had considered another of Caleb's medications, Banzel to be a possible culprit in the Aplastic Anemia battle, but from what Hematology had mentioned, and what I had researched, I doubted this was the answer either, but rather the myelodysplastic syndrome.

His seizures were around the 350 mark daily, his respiratory issues continued to worsen, his GI was full of C Diff and he would cry if you touched his belly. One day while helping me change a C Diff diaper, Peyton said, "Mama, I can't stand it when he cries." and I told her I was with her. She knew as well as all of us, that it had to be terrible for Caleb to cry, and it broke her heart, it broke all of our hearts. Both of the girls hurt badly for their brother. They were wonderful at helping with all the diapers, and Camille especially liked helping me with all his respiratory routine.

We had an appointment with Dr. Moore in respiratory the next week and he said he "didn't like where this was going," when I spoke to him about his overall health. We were holding steady in respiratory, but not having a major improvement, however, he could tell that we were uncomfortable about where Caleb was, and he was on the ball getting us help. He spoke with Radiology Intervention and had them to change out Caleb's GJ tube while we were there to see if it would help with pain at all. He also talked to Hematology for us and let us know that after the last round of blood work, they wanted to do a repeat bone marrow biopsy on the following Monday.

The GJ tube change was extremely painful for Caleb, I about cried myself, but they were quick and wonderful with him and we made it through. I hoped that this would help, it couldn't hurt. However, retching continued and pain continued every time we attached feeds or did his meds or gave him water. It was heartbreaking.

Thursday, December 16th, 2010, Caringbridge entry:

Team Caleb----

Not sure where I should start...today has been a whirlwind....

This morning Beth called GI with her concerns for Caleb, he has been retching(trying to vomit, but since he has the nissian,

nothing can/will come up) continually for the past few nights. She had pulled all his feeds, and tried a line of pedialite, with no change. He is even retching on his meds(which are G fed only) He is unable to produce a BM without an enema and lots of miralax. In addition to all of this he has been in bed since his Bone Marrow Biopsy on Monday. He has slept in bed for over 72 hours, waking only briefly for a few minutes and then back to sleep. Beth explained all of this to Dr. Anderson(GI) around 1 today to which she replied," you have done all you can do at home, bring him in" Rachel sat with him while we packed the car up and we headed out.

Caleb did fine with everything, X-rays, 3 blood drawls, cath/stool sample...the whole nine yards. The last time they drew his blood, he moaned and cried some. To those who know Caleb personally, you know how heartbreaking it is to hear...since he is completely non-verbal, it is just awful to hear him in pain. Beth and I had to suck it up a few times to keep from a meltdown, I cant tell you how rough it was......

He was given IV fluids and has his meds on schedule but with nothing in his stomach he is still retching, and it is just horrible to watch. He is so weak and so pale, he cant hold his head up, or move his arms or legs, and he is so exhausted he is unable to put his hands in his mouth, which is his normal comfort. He just has no energy left, and with the C-Diff still in him, he is zapped.

His blood work for tonight showed more of the same, his hemoglobin is down further, and they will talk to hematology

in the morning about a blood transfusion. We suspect they will NOT want to do one since they still don't know what the cause of the failing bone marrow or neutropenia is.
At this point Beth agrees with them about waiting.

As with everything in Caleb's little life, there are no quick fixes. He has been admitted to room 7421. For now we are just waiting to see if they can figure out a way to allow him to receive his feeds again without retching, his Ketogenic/starvation diet isn't much, and when you don't even get that, well....its just a bad thing all around.

Caleb is a tough little guy, its amazing with what his poor body has been through he has any fight left, but he is a trooper. And equally amazing is how Sis has managed to stay one step ahead of it all.
Life is so precious and things can change in an instant, hug your sweet kiddos extra tight tonight!

We have had tons of calls, emails, inboxes, FB comments, texts....and we love you all for your support. Thank you all for the prayers. Knowing so many are praying and lifting him up to our Lord, is a comfort.
Love to all----
Aunt Ellen

Monday, December 20th, 2010, Caringbridge entry:

Team Caleb,

We are still at Vandy, but working toward coming home. We are so grateful to the team here who are helping us through all these tough decisions but have let us know it is the best thing for Caleb.

It has been very difficult to see him suffer for a long time. We have been trying to make him comfortable, but sometimes in trying to "fix" problems that he is dealing with, we are only putting him through more pain and opening doors to more illness/problems.

He has been so tough for so long and has been so strong and adapted to whatever situation he faces. He is such a good boy, and so precious to us. He may have a long time yet with us, but none of us are promised tommorrow.

So, the plan right now is to do the following:
1. Neurology is starting him on a new medication called "Vigabitrin". We will start it and hope that it will replace the Banzel that we have lost. However, this medication can also reduce RBC's and some of his other meds lower WBC's. So even if it is the Banzel his blood counts may not recover. Dr. Barnes will continue to work closely with us to manage seizures. We still have maximum seizure control as a goal. Dr. Barnes is a dear friend to us at this point and we are so grateful to have him continue with us on this journey with Caleb.
2. Dietary/GI is changing his formula to a more "elemental"

form of diet that may be easier on his GI system. Our sweet Mary Montgomery is walking us through this and will still aid us in finding the right balance for Caleb's nutritional needs.
3. Hematology will give us a report on their findings from the bone marrow that was sent off as soon as they receive it. Their findings may still be inconclusive. However, we are not pursuing any aggressive measures in this department.
4. Genetics is doing a blood draw tommorrow. Caleb has never had an official genetic work up. This may give us insight if some kind of congenital defect has caused Caleb's rapid decline, and may tell us more definitively what we can expect/do for him. If something does come back, it will also give our other children the ability to consider this in their future families. If nothing comes back, then that's ok too. Their research may help some other child in the future.
5. Hospice will be set up at home and our coordination team is working hard to get those supports in place. This is not an easy transition to decide to make, but it truly is best for Caleb. They will aid us in making him comfortable and as pain free as possible. They are also working with Dr. Barnes to set up an "at home" kit for Status Epilepticus, which Caleb has already dealt with twice this year. This will keep us from having to go to the hospital at home to attempt to stop a prolonged seizure.

While all this is difficult we know that God is in control of Caleb's life and that Caleb has been telling us for some time now that he is tired. We are listening to his body and trusting that God will let him be with us as long as He wills. God doesn't always heal those who are ill. Paul asked Christ to heal him of his disease and here was his response:

II Corinthians 12: 9And he said unto me, My grace is sufficient for thee: for my strength is made perfect in weakness. Most gladly therefore will I rather glory in my infirmities, that the power of Christ may rest upon me.
10Therefore I take pleasure in infirmities, in reproaches, in necessities, in persecutions, in distresses for Christ's sake: for when I am weak, then am I strong.

This passage lets us know that even in infirmities, illness, sufferings, that through those weaknesses, Christ's strength will carry us through.

I know that my faith has grown stronger because of having Caleb in our lives. I am so proud of how he has touched the lives of others and continues to. We are so blessed and so grateful to have such beautiful children. Caleb continues to be strong, so we will stand strong with him. But we will no longer let him suffer. He deserves that. He deserves peace and comfort and love.

He is having a tough night tonight, he is seizing in clustered tonics. We are hoping the new meds will kick in quickly and curb this cycle. We expect him to be very tired the next few days, but are hoping to be home for Christmas. I cannot tell you all how thankful we are, for your prayers, notes, cards, words of support and your love. We are overwhelmed, humbled and grateful.

**Love to all of you,
Beth**

We finally got the "ok" and someone at Vandy pushed the "dismiss" button for us, and we got home just in time for Christmas. It seemed like Christmas in some ways, but in so many it didn't. Mostly because the gravity of the situation with Caleb was in the forefront of every day. Caleb was so weak he couldn't do anything but lay and rest. Our friend, Rachel came to Christmas at Nana and Papa's so that he would be safe in the other room with her while we opened presents and visited with the rest of the family. Adding more medications to his schedule and managing it was all consuming, but we had many hands to help us get it going as soon as we got settled.

<u>Medication List for Caleb Baker as of 12/24/10</u>
5AM-   2mg Zofran
         200 mg topamax
         125 mg Dilantin
         200mg gabapentin
6AM- 22.5mg tranxene
         20mg Omeprazole
         50 mg vimpat
          5mg zyrtec
          250 mg Vigabitrin/ 500 mg after 27th
          1ml carnitor sf
          2mls Reglan
11AM- 2 mg Zofran

	2 mls Reglan
	200 mg topamax
12 PM	2.5 mg melatonin
1 PM-	22.5 mg tranxene
	125mg Dilantin
	200 gabapentin
4PM-	2 mls Reglan
5PM-	1 cap mirolax
	200 mg topamax
7PM-	2 mg Zofran
9 PM-	22.5mg.tranxene
	125 mg Dilantin
	50 mg vimpat
	5mg singulair
	5mg melatonin
	1 ml carnitor sf
	2mls Reglan
	250 vigabitrin/ 500 mg after 27th
11PM-	200 gabapentin
	200 mg topamax

(This is a listing of Caleb's daily schedule of meds and was typical of the ever changing regimen he kept over the years.)

The rest of our time for Christmas was spent at home. I allowed the family that had come in to mask up and come and see him for a few moments.

Our Hospice nurses came to see us on December 28th, and set up care for Caleb. One of them, Laura Griffith had been praying for Caleb for a long time. (He was on more prayer lists than I could even imagine). She had also been following him on Caringbridge, her best friend had been one of Caleb's OT's and her mother in law was one of Caleb's aides back in preschool! They gave us lots of information and prepared us for things that would be needed, such as setting up oxygen at home and discussed feeds.

Caleb had not been tolerating his feeds for some while. The only reason he was tolerating the little that he was receiving was because of the pain medication added to his regimen. He was very uncomfortable at times still. It was heartbreaking, feeding is a maternal instinct. I had accepted the fact that I was unable to "feed him" two years prior to this point. However, the fact that the trickle of feeds and the small amount of meds we were giving him were too much for him was just not good.

His bowels slowed, his pain became more evident. He had problems with running low grade temperatures off and on. His seizures had thankfully slowed down with the spike in temperature, so it was a welcome short break.

Our nurse let us know if we wanted to do anything with Caleb or get away that we needed to do it. We considered several options, but decided he wasn't really well enough to do anything. We were grateful for the past year of trips that we had made with him, and decided to just let him rest at home, where he was most comfortable.

Caleb's pain was so intense. I spoke to Laura, our nurse about his feeds. I knew in my heart, that he was not able to tolerate them at all. I prayed that God would guide me in what to do for Caleb. I needed Caleb to tell me somehow what to do for him. On Monday night, January 10th, Caleb had a terrible night of pain. I knew it was his way of telling me he was finished hurting. It was hard to come to the decision to remove his feeds, they were keeping him alive- but they were causing him unbelievable pain. Chad and I discussed this with Laura. She supported us and let us know that we were doing the right thing for him. The feeds were there for us, not for Caleb, and I had to tell myself that to be able to unplug the line from his mic-key for the last time, on January 11th.

We let the girls know what would happen. They wept. We wept. We had fought for so long to try to keep Caleb with us, that giving control of the situation over to him and listening to what his body was telling us was hard to do.

Our family surrounded us, and were there around the clock. A candlelight vigil and sweet friends stood outside of our home on Wednesday the 12th. They sang the "I love you" Barney song, and "Jesus loves Me" and Caleb's dear friend, Grant Eyer, was right there leading them. It was precious.

The girls came home from school early on Thursday the 13th. We felt it was best for them to be at home as Caleb's throat and lung noises and breathing had changed rapidly. He was not awake very much, so it was so precious when the girls came in and he opened his eyes when he heard them talking. Our Hospice nurse, Laura switched to continual care that afternoon.

Friday the house was full of our immediate families. My Mama and Daddy (Nana and Papa), Chad's mom (Gran), and all my siblings and their families. At 8 pm we started letting each of them go in and say their goodbyes if they wished. It was the toughest thing to watch people tell your child goodbye. Our girls were so brave. They both went into the room with Caleb by themselves. They came out and we embraced them and reassured them of what wonderful sisters they were to their little brother. It was so hard. There was just no way for me to know what they were going through in being a child yourself and losing someone who was a child. But they were brave and strong and we were so proud of them, and still are, they are amazing girls.

Our nurse sat in the bedroom with us, Caleb, Chad and I, as I asked her to and she would slip out from time to time to tell the family how things were. Caleb's eyes had been closed for many hours. He was pale and weak. He hadn't moved for a long time. He continued to have myoclonic seizures. His breath slowed. At 1:07 am Saturday, he opened his eyes and looked at Chad, then he heard my voice saying, "It's okay sweet boy, you can go." and turned and looked at me one last time with those precious beautiful big brown eyes.

We cried over his weakening body. His coloring began to change, his breathing was labored.

At 4:20 am, while laying in my arms, Caleb's heart stopped beating. His eyes opened, and his spirit left his body, and we gave him back to God. It was the worst moment of my life, but in that same moment, it was the most joyous day of Caleb's. For now, he was in Heaven, free from pain, free from struggles, free from seizures.

Caringbridge entry Saturday January 15th, 2011:

Team Caleb----

Our sweet boy went to eternal peace this morning at 4:20. He was resting in his mother's arms, and his daddy by his side.

Around 8 last evening our great hospice nurse, Laura, had us to spend time with him individually. We all took our turns saying goodbye, and the girls went in last before Beth and Chad. I am so proud of those girls, they love their little brother so much and they have been such wonderful sisters to him. His breathing was labored and pulse was low, but his fight was still strong, it always has been.

Beth and Chad stayed alone by his side from around 9 on. a little after 1 this morning Beth said he opened his eyes and looked straight at Chad, who told him it was okay to go, and then he turned to look at Beth. She reassured him that it was okay. That moment was hard on them, but so touching,......His little body was built strong. He was not in pain and we are so blessed to know he went peacefully.
Beth and Chad are strong and carried him one last time out of the house.

Our hearts are broken but we rejoice with the angels in heaven, for we know he is finally without seizures, and where there is no pain, no suffering, and no sorrow.

We wish we could see his happy face and sweet voice singing with Jesus now, and we long for that day to be with him again. He has loved ones there to welcome him, and endless Barney to enjoy. I bet his little legs have not stopped running since he flew home. What a ball of energy he is right now.......

We thank you all for your endless prayers, they have carried us all.

We praise God for having a placed prepared for our sweet Bubba.....and we know he is free.

Love to all----
Aunt Ellen

Chapter 17: Lessons from Caleb's Journey

There are so many things that flood your heart in grief. There was a terrible emptiness that permeates you physically, I could just feel that loss right in my heart. I ached. We all ached.

But Caleb had been taking baby steps backward for years, little tiny steps away from this world, so that slowly, I and his loved ones, could let him go back to God. He taught me more in his short little life than years of education have brought. His life taught me lessons of patience, longsuffering, joy, kindness, and hope.

There are times that I remember just thinking "why us", "why my child", however, it didn't last long, because I knew in my heart that God chose me to be Caleb's mother for a reason. God only gives us what we can handle, it is how we deal with it that allows us to become either weak, or strong.

I knew my Caleb was a fighter, and I refused to let any diagnosis or any inability to define his being. We accepted whatever it was and moved on. I remember the heartache over learning he was dealing with Autism. I remember the grief that ensued. It was tough, there is no denying that. But knowing that your child is dealing with something that you are going to have to help them through should give you strength to persevere. There is no time for a pity party for yourself, you can have about 5 minutes, and then you have to pick yourself up and start helping your child.

It makes your life easier to be determined to help them through whatever it is they are dealing with, you are not the victim, they are. When Caleb passed away, Laura told me I had two days and then she was coming to get me if I wasn't "up and going." I didn't take two days. I didn't stay in bed one day, I cried myself to sleep at night while reliving Caleb's final moments over and over in my mind. I guess this was an attempt to make it seem real, but also, because it was his life that was gone, not mine. My whole world had changed in that moment on January 15th. My life had been devoted to him, almost solely. It took every moment of my day and night to care for him and make sure his needs were met. So now, without him, I would have to learn how to live again.

I want to share with you what Caleb taught me.

Never Give Up

Caleb never did. If there was a truck he wanted to play with and he couldn't make his hands work to pick it up, he would find a way with his feet! He had an unusual way of going about things, but it worked for him.

We fought seizures until the last moments of his life. We struggled to keep Caleb comfortable on a daily basis, but through all of that discomfort, he continued to find a way from time to time, to SMILE.

There is nothing in this world worth giving up over. Caleb

continued to fight through pain, illness, seizures, and he never complained. I know verbally, he could not. But even if he could have, I don't believe he would have. He accepted whatever change was brought his way, he went from bacon to g-tube feeds without ever breaking down in front of the microwave. He dealt with whatever illness came along. He was patient with me. He knew I would work hard to get his needs met. He knew we were fighting for him.

There are many trials in life. There are times when nothing goes your way. There are moments of grief, pain, sadness, loss, illness and anger. But trials are just building blocks to making you a better person. There is always a way to find happiness and contentment wherever you are in life. You just have to find it. That is the battle. Don't let things in life's journey bring your spirit down. You can go on. Never give up.

Fight For Your Child

As adults, there is plenty of stress, worry and strife to consume your day. But children cannot fight for themselves when they have problems- as a parent- to fight for your children- that is your job.

I cannot say how much Caleb has changed my perspective on most things. There is a look that he would give you that would just melt your heart. Through his struggles, there was one thing that is evident, NO ONE will fight for your child unless YOU DO.

If you are determined to help your child, so will others. You must lead the team. You must carry the load. You must organize, plan, chart, and lead the team in hope. If you don't your child will not overcome whatever it is that they are facing. But if you lead, others will get on board, and you will help your child to fight against the odds.

We were very blessed to have had excellent teachers, therapists and doctors in Caleb's life. We had many who got on board and helped him along his way. There were others who took the "He can't" attitude. They quickly either were shown how he could, or they were no longer part of the team. Your job as a parent is to find a way that HE CAN, and teach the teachers, therapists, doctors or even your own family to understand that they have to focus on the positive and find every opportunity to make the child successful. That is the key.

One day can bring a monumental amount of change with a child with ASD or Epilepsy. But meeting the child wherever he is, every day and taking it a day, sometimes even a moment at a time is the best way to overcome daily stresses, and will free you to see the positive.

I can remember thinking I could not stand to watch the Doodlebops one more time one day. I know we had seen the same episode at least 5 times. But then, Caleb smiled and I let him watch it 2 more times in hopes that he would smile again. I would have watched it forever if he would have smiled.

Move past pessimism, open your heart and listen to it. Many times you will see the things your child cannot do, but try to open your eyes to things that they can do. Open your heart to accepting your child for who they are, and what they can be.

Caleb could not do many things. My hopes for him were shattered, the worry of him not getting well could have consumed us. But you have to move past these things and give your child the one thing your child needs the most---YOU.

Look For The Good

Boy is this world full of bad. Ugly looks at Wal-mart need to become the least of your worries. Your job is your child. Learn not to care what others say/think/do. That's a tall order, but if you focus on your child you will save yourself a lot of heartache over it. My decision to think to myself: "they are unlearned", got me past lots of stares. There were moments we would be places and Caleb would scream or cry. My job was to make him either comfortable wherever we were, or to get him out of the situation. So if you are unable to use tools to calm them- leave. Wal-mart can always wait. Your child can not.

If someone offers to help you, let them. This is difficult to do. I have had an amazing amount of people to bring us gestures of concern and love. When someone wants to do good, then find them something they can help you do. Let them come fold your laundry or cook a meal, or run your other children to their activities. Whatever it is, let them help you. Don't find what they can't do, find them something they can.

You cannot have good in your life if you don't look for it. Some days are easy. You see wonderful progress, or a beautiful smile. Those days are easy to see the good. I am talking about the tough days- the days when things are at the breaking point. The days like we had everyone covered in Cdiff on the parking lot of Disney World, you have to look for good, because there was nothing good going on in the moment. Until I about broke down, then I looked at my girls who were standing at the ready to help, and that was the good, and we made it through it. You just have to go on, no matter what, because for your child- you must.

LOVE

Love can overcome anything. I never loved Autism or Epilepsy, but I loved Caleb more because of how he dealt with these struggles. Love transcends illness. So many times there are people around us, right next to us, that you would never know are dealing with terrible illness, loss, or devastating circumstances. Find a way to reach out. Find a way to love them through the awful struggles that they face. Life is not easy. Life is not fair. But life is a test of how much you can LOVE.

Children with illness teach us how we should view life. We should live with love in our hearts. We should be forgiving spirits. We should be patient, joyful, faithful, kind, longsuffering, peaceful and good. Matthew 19:14 "But Jesus said, Suffer little children, and forbid them not, to come unto me: for of such is the kingdom of heaven."

Love for others is seeing past yourself and wanting good to come to all around you. Do you have a family member with illness? Do you help? Do you educate yourself on what they are dealing with? Do you criticize what the family is doing? Or do you lift them up? Do you love them enough to give of your time? Do you see them in Wal-mart and run down the other aisle to avoid them? Don't run away. Families with children with special needs, they need your love. If you love them the way you should, you will help them. You can offer to run errands. You can become a respite provider for them. You can fold their laundry, clean house, take them supper. It is lifelong for them, it is not just a week of illness, it is a lifetime. You have the opportunity to reach out, to lighten their load and to show them your love. Do it. You will bless them, and they will bless your life too. Love them.

Find Happiness in the Small Things

There were so many things that Caleb was unable to do. And sometimes, finding something that could make him happy was very difficult. Caleb had learned to watch "The Heffalump Movie." He had a favorite part where the little purple elephant, the Heffalump, would sing a cute little song and jumped around. When Caleb watched this, on a good day, he might smile at it. But, on a great day, he would laugh a little when we sang it with and danced his little stuffed Heffalump around. It was the most precious thing. It usually didn't last long, and after you'd done it once or twice, you would get no reaction at all. But just being able to make that connection with him, to be silly and get a smile or even better a bit of a laugh was the most amazing reward that could last me all day, and sometimes, it had to last a week or more. There were days when there was nothing that we could do to break through and get to Caleb, but for the moments that we could it was a true blessing. He found moments of happiness in small things, and we had to learn to as well.

The last words I ever heard Caleb say were in October of 2007. I was lifting him out of the back of the car, and typically I would say "Come to Mommy" in an attempt to have him lean toward me so I could get him out of his carseat. Caleb's words were very seldom able to be accessed by him at this point, and our communication was usually by non-verbal cues. That day, he leaned forward and said "Mommy hold you." I have lived on those words for over three years now. Three little words, that somehow made a connection that day and were graciously given to me from his sweet little voice. Those words meant so much to me, I hoped that he knew: he could depend on me, he knew I was going to be there to carry him, he knew I would support him, he knew I loved him.

It was the last thing he ever said to me. When he died, I held him in my arms. And I promised him that someday "Mommy will hold you again." Knowing that I can't right now, it makes me sad. But those three little words he said to me, they resonate in my heart every day.

When you face struggles, and you will, find something simple that makes you happy, and think about that and be grateful. There are days of terrible grief, pain and suffering on this earth. Everyone around us has trials and tribulations, that is a fact of life. But finding some way to find happiness in the small things can carry you through. Caleb was able to find small things that would warm his heart and make him smile, not every day, but along the journey from time to time. We are so thankful for every little smile we were so blessed to see.

Live For Your Child

This one is tough. Caleb is gone. I must go on. It is tough to know that I was unable to help him. I know his doctors and all of our family felt the same way, it is a tremendous blow to fight so hard and to not be able to save a child. We are so blessed in this country to have many ways to fight illnesses. Caleb was not meant to be here to continue suffering. He was meant to be here for a time with us and then to end suffering and gain Heaven. It was tough for me to deal with letting him go.

But life is about loss. From the moment you are born, the dying process begins. What you do during that time, is your journey. Caleb's journey is a beautiful one. His life was full of bad, but he made it good. He made others good. He brought beauty and grace and love and happiness to all around him through the midst of illness.

After Caleb's death, the consensus between doctors and my

research led us to believe that Caleb had some form of multi-system disease. He passed away before we were able to do final tests that could have confirmed a possible mitochondrial dysfunction, but many medical issues he dealt with mimicked that. Regardless of what the official underlying diagnosis would have been, the inevitable loss would have been the same.

Caleb was able to live with moments of joy even in the midst of pain. He taught others to love those that were different than themselves. He taught us to never give up, to fight, to look for the good, to find happiness, to love and to live.

I will continue my life in helping other families like ours, with children with ASD and Epilepsy, who truly are blessings to the world. The weakest among us are the strongest, for they cause us all to reflect on our lives and cause us to become better people. I will help others who are dealing with grief- an ongoing process throughout our lives with Caleb. I am a better person because of Caleb, his journey lives on through me. Every day we are faced with choices, every day is full of blessings and trials, strength and moments of weakness. But one thing we can do is be determined to make a difference in the life of another. Caleb taught me to BE THE BLESSING.

Facts about Epilepsy

Epilepsy affects over 3 million Americans of all ages – more than multiple sclerosis, cerebral palsy, muscular dystrophy, and Parkinson's disease combined.

Almost 500 new cases of epilepsy are diagnosed every day in the United States. Epilepsy affects 50,000,000 people worldwide.

In two-thirds of patients diagnosed with epilepsy, the cause is unknown.

Epilepsy can develop at any age and can be a result of genetics, stroke, head injury, birth defects, and many other factors, many of them being unknown.

In over thirty percent of patients, seizures cannot be controlled with treatment.

Uncontrolled seizures may lead to brain damage and death.

The severe epilepsy syndromes of childhood can cause developmental delay and brain damage, leading to a lifetime of dependency and continually accruing costs.

It is estimated that up to 50,000 deaths occur annually in the U.S. from status epilepticus (prolonged seizures), Sudden Unexplained Death in Epilepsy (SUDEP), and other seizure-related causes such as drowning and other accidents.

The mortality rate among people with epilepsy is two to three times higher than the general population and the risk of sudden death is twenty-four times greater.

Recurring seizures are also a burden for those living with brain tumors and other disorders such as cerebral palsy, mental retardation, and autism.

Families who have members with Epilepsy need extra support from their extended family, friends and community to be able to cope with the daily stresses brought upon them and their loved one.

Stats about Caleb:
Caleb's condition of diffuse bilateral cortical dysplasia is extremely rare.

There are 2 types of seizures: Generalized (or what people call Grand-Mal) or Partial Seizures (Petit-Mal) Underneath these two types, there are subtypes. Caleb had both generalized seizures and partial seizures.

Some of the kinds of generalized seizures are: Tonic, Tonic-Clonic, Gelastic, Frontal-Lobe, Absence, and Myoclonic. Caleb experienced all of these.

Caleb generally experienced 100 seizures daily. He has had as many as 1200 seizures in a day, and as few as 30 in a day.

Caleb had been on over 14 anticonvulsants to try to help his seizures cease.
The TOTAL numbers reflect total seizures seen and charted during 2008, 2009, 2010 and the last month of his life, January of 2011. Adding numbers from 2006, and 2007, Caleb experienced over 157,000 seizures that were visible.

Seizure Log Caleb Baker 2010

Month	myoclonic	tonic	totals
Jan.	965	264	1231
Feb.	880	132	1038
Mar.	1465	125	1655
Apr.	2670	291	3108
May.	2175	296	2559
Jun.	2200	201	2845
Jul.	1590	264	2825
Aug.	2520	349	4337
Sept.	5290	382	8055
Oct.	7135	587	9929
Nov.	7940	105	10955+
Dec.	2820	662	7017
Jan. 2011	1400	91	2230
TOTAL	130880	11629	156312

www.ingramcontent.com/pod-product-compliance
Lightning Source LLC
Chambersburg PA
CBHW032120090426
42743CB00007B/410